*From a*
*Listening Heart*

Now King Solomon went to Gibeon . . . that
night the Lord God appeared to him in a dream
and said, 'What shall I give you? Tell me.'
And Solomon answered, . . . 'Give thy servant . . .
a heart with skill to listen' . . .

I Kings 3:4ff, The New English Bible

# From a Listening Heart

∽∽∽∽

JACK L. MOORE

DOUBLEDAY & COMPANY, INC.

GARDEN CITY, NEW YORK

1975

Some of the stories in *From a Listening Heart* are revisions of articles earlier published in the Presbyterian *Survey,* official magazine of the Presbyterian Church in the United States, and are used with permission.

Library of Congress Cataloging in Publication Data

Moore, Jack L   1920–
    From a listening heart.

    1. Meditations.   I. Title.
BV4832.2.M567     242
ISBN 0-385-08422-6
Library of Congress Catalog Card Number 74–31517

*First Edition*

*To All of You*

# CONTENTS

*When I was four years old, my*
*daddy used to pick me up and put me*
*on the back of a gentle old mare. Then*
*I'd ride three miles to town and get*
*the mail. Somebody there would take me off*
*the horse and put me back on.*

*My life has always been filled with*
*people willing to give me a lift up.*

*Jack L. Moore*

*From a
Listening Heart*

# ROOM TO BE ME

The morning is hot. Texas hot with not one tiny breeze to move the heat around.

The sweat of my brow is considerable. But nothing to compare with the buckets of perspiration dripping from the rest of me.

Pausing from my weed chopping to eavesdrop on a friendly bee whispering sweet nothings to an uncaring and indifferent broccoli plant, I marveled at the magnificence of my garden.

Oh, not that it's all that big. About two hundred square feet squeezed between the garage and the alley. And it's not even impressive looking.

You know, it's just a garden. A little of this and a little of that. Infiltrated by Dallis grass and Johnson grass and a bunch of other unwelcome weeds with lesser pedigrees.

Yet, it is producing so much for me. Let me tell you.

To begin with, it wasn't really a serious venture. Fed up to here with inflation and all the political double-talk about, I decided to put in a vegetable garden. Then I could righteously point out that I was doing something besides griping and complaining.

You guessed it! This garden is a flat miracle. In spite of all I could do, it has prospered from the beginning. Tomatoes are running out of our ears and there's plenty of lettuce, string beans, lima beans and a little corn.

And even my failures looked good while striking out. Two rows of sturdy, healthy broccoli plants grew and grew and grew but never got around to having any little broccolis. And the squash. You should have seen it. From each plant there came beautiful golden blossoms, one after the other. They bloomed and flourished and withered away. Giving birth to a single squash, about the size of an underdeveloped pickle.

Most impressive of all, however, were the creepers growing out from melon seed imported from Israel. Those things are starting to get scary. They've crawled around the squash, through the corn and are now heading for my neighbor's back yard. But no melons!

Standing and dripping, I'm thinking.

That this garden offers me something more. Some time-tested knowledge dealing with my relationship with God. Having to do with my fellowship with you. Speaking to my accepting and getting along with me.

Watching the parched, thirsty soil, day after day, soak up streams of life-giving and life-saving water, I am reminded of my own infinite need for nurture.

Seeing the confusion and some of the retarded growth caused by my crowding everything together in an effort to save space, I am faced with a basic truth. Everything and everyone needs room to be. You need room to be you. I need room to be me. Maybe we'll remember when next we start crowding each other!

Marveling over the way some things flourished and grieving over the demise of others, it dawned on me that it was my failure to know more about what I was doing that was mostly to blame. I knew a little but wouldn't, didn't take time to study up on the fine points. You'll more likely thrive in my garden if I will make an honest effort to get to know you. Intimacy is never superficial.

Threaded in the picture and tied to the message is this.

There were some quiet morning times, while the sun was chinning on the horizon, when I watched a new sprout pushing through the earth's crust like a baby chick shrugging out of an egg.

Like me. Buried in the darkness and finally breaking through to light.

And I gloried.

In the excitement and joy of being part of a miracle.

The miracle of God's creation.

Lord, for the zest of living and the hooray of being
brought to new life in Christ, I give you a toast
with the wine of my soul.
Amen.

# A DAY FOR THE LORD

There are days that pass and are soon forgotten. Remembered only as a tiny grain of sand in the midst of the dunes that edge the shores of my life.

Then there are other days. Days that are eventfully marked. Significantly singled out. Perhaps by a milestone that is a tribute to what has gone before and a promise of what is still to come.

Or set apart by happenings that stoke my emotions and stir feelings from the depth of my being.

This was such a day.

I remember vaguely crawling into bed, very late, and trying to stay awake long enough to pray. It wasn't much of a prayer. Lord, I murmured, thank you for seeing me through the day and for making me know and accept that you love me.

Probably that was enough.

Surely he knew how tired I was. How bone-tired and emotionally drained.

You understand, don't you, what I'm talking about? You know that feeling. You've been there.

That's why I wanted to share the day with you.

It had wound down that evening with me in a swimming pool. Doggedly paddling from side to side. Trying to ease the muscle cramp in the back of my neck. Seeking to untangle the nerves knotted with tension.

But maybe I ought to start at the start.

Awake before dawn, I waited to first light before fixing the coffee and easing out on the patio to get myself ready for the day. But I wonder. Do you ever get ready, really get ready for such a day?

My first task was the most heart wrenching.

I drove the youngest of my sons to the airport and saw him off to a far country. Only a week out of high school, he was joining a railroad work crew on the East Coast, not to return until the fall. And then he'll be home just long enough to get launched to another far country for college. For life.

I'm not going to lie about it. I died a little inside. Remembering too many memories and hurting with each flashback, I watched that airplane become a speck and disappear. And still I couldn't cry. Just kept swallowing. Bitterness.

Only an hour or so later, I spoke for a funeral.

Talked about victory over death and believed what I said. But still pondered and pondered. Remembering the desolation that sweeps over me whenever someone near and dear has died.

Then, just a few hours afterward, I was the officiant for a wedding. A happy time, you say? Perhaps, but still a reminder that the demands of relationships are most intense in the fragile bonds of marriage. A time of wondering and hoping and praying.

Just remembering that day brings a tightening of my jaws. A feeling of tension creeping in once more.

But it was a great day.

A day for the Lord.

Without him, it could not have been. For me.

For that young son.

For that old man.

For the loving couple.

All launching new lives.

O God, grant me willingness to share my heart with you, that your heart may save my life for me.

Amen.

# FOR SCOFFERS

It was about dusk, she explained.

She was just leaving the drive-in grocery in her neighborhood when she was approached by a young man.

He was barefooted. His hair was long. So long he had it tied in a pigtail and it was hanging down his back. Almost to his waist. He had on a faded blue denim jacket and jeans. Clean, but showing signs of age and hard wearing.

He simply walked up to her and asked for a ride. Actually, he was more specific than that. He wanted to be taken to a particular place, a street intersection that was several miles out of her way.

Didn't seem the least bit bashful, she said. Looked her full in the face and asked, Will you drive me out to where Apple Street crosses Miller Road?

She was alone.

The only people were inside the store. There was hardly any traffic.

Nervously, she admits, she returned his look. Glanced around, then looked again at his face. Into his eyes. Finally, with reservations but a strange sense of confidence, she agreed to take him.

Knowing her, I'm not all that surprised.

Nor does it come as a surprise to learn they carried on an animated, personal kind of conversation during their trip. She is the sort who enjoys talking. With the kind of openness that invites, maybe even demands, response.

I'm not sure how far they drove, nor how long it took. But it was far enough. And long enough.

As I said, their conversation was not ordinary. They didn't discuss the weather. Or how pretty it was with the sun setting and all. It was about living and dying. Risking and searching. Absolutes and ultimates.

Just before they reached his appointed destination, he told her. Who he was. At least, he told her who he claimed he was.

I am Jesus the Christ, he said.

Later, when she had let him out of the car and was on her way home, she was sorting out her feelings.

If he really is Jesus, she giggled uneasily, I sure am glad I gave him a ride.

It's easy to scoff.

To snort in contempt and to know all about the long-haired "nuts" that are running around in the world today.

To rail and fuss at anybody, male or female, who is stupid enough or silly enough or crazy enough to take a stranger into their car. Or their home. Or their hearts.

Most probably, we scoffers and snorters have right and reason lined up solidly behind us. Statistics prove it is a dangerous practice. And, after all, we do have to draw the line somewhere. There is a limit to how far we're supposed to go in helping a person in need. There's our own security and safety to be considered. And properly.

But I have to wonder.

When He came. Riding that lowly ass. Probably barefooted and long-haired. In no way appearing as the King of kings.

I have to wonder.

How many of those hurrying to their homes or to their work or to wherever. How many of those even noticed Him?

And how many of those who bothered to look a second time at the stranger on a donkey. How many of those believed?

And how many others scoffed and snorted?

And still do!

# OLD DREAMS

Back yonder a few years, before the days of interstates and incredible Mixmasters and loops around loops, taking an automobile trip was a lot more adventuresome. Well, maybe what I mean is that it was a different sort of adventure.

Nowadays, you know, driving 55 to 65 miles per hour in a heavy, high-powered car over a long, straight stretch of interstate is as exciting as discussing the weather with your in-laws.

Your eyes get heavy and your right foot gets heavier and the next thing you know, you are jerking yourself awake and the needle of the speedometer is hovering around 90. Which is a sudden way to go. A little more sudden than I have in mind.

Well, I want to tell you a simple way to keep this from happening. It's so simple I don't know why I didn't think of it a long time ago.

Just get off the big highways.

That's right. If you're driving a couple of hundred miles or so, start a little earlier. Map a route that follows the farm-to-market roads, or the state roads, or maybe what was once a superhighway before they built the super-dupers. And enjoy!

Doing it that way, you have to watch out for the oncoming traffic, keep one eye peeled for farm machinery and the other one watching for livestock. You'll discover that the road will have a lot of neat little curves with a blind hill or two thrown in for excitement. Once in awhile, if you're really lucky, you may even wind up on an old-fashioned gravel road and be treated to a washboard ride.

One thing for sure. A day of that kind of driving and you won't have to be rocked to sleep.

Adding some extra zest to travel on back roads is the possible probability of taking a wrong fork or discovering too late that your road map has been purposely doctored. But, listen, getting lost may be the most fun thing that happens on your whole trip. I've personally discovered that sleeping beside a pasture filled with friendly cows is a lot better than watching television in an overpriced motel.

By now, I'll bet you've recognized that the last time I was on such a trip I came across a provocative thought. And that I am working around to sharing this with you.
If I don't get all turned around.
On one of the back roads of my mind.

My sharing is not something I learned. It's more like an observation, fringed with a kind of wondering.
This particular back road had, at one time, been the main thoroughfare. Going for hundreds of miles and always right through the middle of the little towns it connected. Which means it's pretty old, and with age comes potholes and washouts and whocares. That makes driving something you do slowly and carefully or your car winds up with a broken axle and you wind up very sore.
That's what made the trip so neat. Driving slowly I had time to notice, to really see, things that would have been an uninteresting blur if I had been doing business as usual.
What I mainly noticed were old dreams.

About halfway between towns, at the junction of a narrow blacktop that ambles across a cotton field, sits a half-finished concrete block church. Stopping for a closer look, I found a sign that only teases my imagination.
This Building Will Be Empty When The Rapture Comes.
I looked inside.
It is empty.

A little farther down the road, I came upon a little abandoned frame store. Wooden porch curtsying to the east. A weathered Brown Mule chewing tobacco sign clinging tentatively to the false front. Dust-streaked broken windows welcoming friendly wasps and busy bumblebees. One long out-dated gasoline pump, tilted slightly to the right, is standing guard duty. And waiting.

Closer in to town is the Elite Motel. Twelve forlorn cabins huddling on a naked hilltop. Broken screens hanging dejectedly and spiders spinning their webs in the unused emptiness. Their only customers, the tumbleweeds that come rolling out of the prairie and find refuge wedged under the corners. Until the blowing winds tear them loose and send them packing.

And there are others. But you get the idea.

I can imagine how it was in the days when the dreams were young and fresh. And hope was a strong tonic.

But, what happened?

Did the dreamers stop dreaming and drift away to wear out the rest of existence?

Or did the end of the old dreams simply mark the beginning of new ones?

How is it with you?

# WORDS

He's a strong, handsome man in his middle years. Tough and independent. A willing and able workman, a pleasant and congenial companion. The sort of fellow I'd like to have with me on a fishing trip, or camping down in the Big Bend country.

Except he can't go.

And maybe never again.

A malignant growth, once only a vague shadow on the back of a lung, has simply exploded. Now, when he looks up from his hospital bed with a smile trembling uneasily around his mouth and his eyes starting to moisten and crinkling with deep emotion. When the unspoken Why of life lunges at me from behind his crumbling dignity.

What word do I speak?

What can I say?

And still another friend, one who is well past the three score and ten standard, sits in the comfort of his old home. Stunned and bewildered.

His beloved wife is dead. For more than half of a century their living has been a duet of great vigor and harmony, accompanied by the warming strains of plain old-fashioned love.

But no more.

The program is changed, and he has no choice. He must go on by himself. A solo. After fifty years, his life is suddenly empty. The hours are slow torture, the days offer painful memories. So he sits and waits. For death.

What word is there in me, for him?

What can I say?

But the need for the right word is not bound to high drama. It's everywhere. And always.

. . . Dad, my confident seventeen-year-old man-son begins, there's an all-night party. A bunch of us are gonna work on the homecoming float. See you later. OK?

. . . Or my beautiful sixteen-year-old, ink still wet on her driver's license, casual and calm. Oh, Pops, it'll be all right if I drive my friends to the late movie, won't it? I told them I would.

. . . Or when the friendly neighborhood TV repairman has driven six blocks and devoted fifteen minutes to replacing the thingamajig in the whatchamacallit and, cheerfully, hands me a bill for $47, including a $6 part, a $25 service charge, and the minimum two-hour labor cost at $8 an hour.

The truth is, my friends, words—the right ones—are never easily come by.

And that childhood litany, the one about sticks and stones, is a tragic falsehood. Words not only can hurt, but they can kill. They can destroy hope and confidence. They can wipe out old friendships and old friends.

Even as they can introduce healing, encourage hoping, and renew our living. Rebuild our vital relationships.

My words, and yours, have a spreading effect. Like rocks tossed into a calm lake cause ripples to chase each other frantically.

Can it be? That casual and indifferent words reflect casual and indifferent people? Who don't really care about other people?

That interested and concerned words reflect interested and concerned people? Who not only care.

But who know in their heart of hearts that God cares.

You know.

That's the word I'm always looking for. It's always right. It's always exactly right.

God's word!

    O God, let the words of my mouth
offer hope and confidence and give fresh
assurance. But only when my life reflects
your word.

# WHO ARE YOU?

Who are you?

Your letter came this morning. So innocent in that plain white envelope. Probably I should have been wary when I noticed, but only casually, there was no return address.

When I opened the envelope and that little half-sheet of typing paper slipped out, it still didn't give me any warning. And, honestly, it took a few moments for the shock of your message to start clawing at my stomach.

Who are you?

Are you the lady whose husband died a few months ago? I remember your talking about the emptiness of your house, and I was thinking that you were really talking about your heart. And there does seem a sort of look in your face that says you could be the one.

Or maybe you're the young girl whose bottom lip was quivering so when you casually mentioned that you don't have any friends among your classmates. But that it doesn't make any difference to you. Remember? You were so insistent that it is much more fun to stay home and play records and watch television. That making friends is a waste of time.

Really, now. Who are you?

Your message came through loud and clear. It's just that I don't know which one you are.

Maybe you are the man who feels your marriage has reached a dead end. How did you say it when you came in to talk? That you keep having this feeling, a recurring nightmare sort of thing, you are trying to walk across a vast desert. Wearing hip boots. That you are literally smothering to death in a relationship that is dull and deadly and dreary. That's right. That's the way you said it.

Or you could be the young divorcee who keeps telling me your life is a bowl of cherries, sitting there waiting for you to eat all you want. But the way you chatter on and on about all the busy things that you do. The way your hands nervously search your purse, touch your hair and fumble with your car keys. A lot of nervous little habits you keep adding to make me wonder. And doubt a little.

Listen, I've been agonizing over your message and I need to know. Who are you?

Are you the person whose eyes are always cast down when we meet and whose hand is always cold to my touch? Or maybe you are the person who seems to look searchingly into my eyes and who squeezes my hand when we greet?

The more I think of it, the more aware I am that you could be almost any one of the hundreds of persons I see and speak to and make an effort to know. Every week.

Whoever you are, will you listen to me for just a little bit? Please?

I know your message is real and your feelings are honest. And I'm not going to pat you on the shoulder and say, There now, there now, don't you fret and don't you cry, everything's going to be all right, in the by and by. You wouldn't want me to be that phony.

But I do have a message for you.

And it comes from my heart.

You are important. You are important to me, to a lot of other people who probably haven't gotten your message. For whatever reason.

Will you do something for me? Right now?

Go into your bedroom and look into your mirror. See there someone who is loved. Someone who has love to give to others. Someone who has a special, unique relationship to God. To yourself. And to the rest of us.

Take a good long look.

Then, by grace, maybe you'll be able to square your shoulders and to hold your head up and maybe you'll smile a little self-conscious smile. And you'll hear me telling you, You are somebody! And I'll hear you whispering, You bet I am!

That won't keep you from being alone. It won't keep you from having feelings of loneliness. But it'll be a step in the right direction. So that your next letter will have a signature.

Instead of being a one-word message. Help.

Signed, One Very Lonely Person.

O God, let us recognize and accept
your value for us that in our worthiness
we will not be afraid. Grant that fearing
and loneliness will not cripple our living.
And our loving.

# ANOTHER KIND OF WINNER

One of the ancient bromides employed by pulpit-pounding football coaches to stir the laggards in their flocks is, "When the going gets tough, the tough get going." The flip side of that sermon is, "Winners don't quit, and quitters don't win."

Along those same lines, my war-time stint in the Marine Corps taught me. Rather, it imbedded in the very depths of my being. That my feelings and my thinking had almost nothing to do with my capacity to perform. I could be so weary I knew my death was only minutes away and the man would say, "Let's go." And I went.

Which isn't all that different from a lot of my learning during the early years of my life. Passed on with diligence by assorted uncles and cousins and town loafers who were all experts. During the many, many fist fights of my boyhood, I recall vividly being egged on by red-necked grown-ups, "Git up and whip'im, boy, y'awl ain't hurt."

By the grace of a loving God and the loving patience of a lot of Godpeople, I am gradually coming to know winning is not the only thing in life. That it's not even the biggest thing.

Whether it's football games, the World Series, wars, kid fights, or arguments with you.

Guess that's why some different things are impressing to me. And some different people.

He hesitatingly said he actually didn't know me. But somebody had told him I was the kind of guy that might listen to his story. He was hoping I would. I did.

It isn't what you would describe as a tragedy. At least, not yet it isn't.

He's better-than-average educated and has considerable talent in his vocation. Very personable. Also he has five children. And no wife.

Without getting into all the details, it can be summed up by saying he's made a lot of crucial errors in his more recent jobs. So now he's out of work. Looking for another chance. He's broke and his children are hungry.

But that's not what this is all about.

Instead, it's a report on the spirit and the attitude of a man hanging on the ropes. He was not looking for a handout, though he surely could use a hand up.

What he needed most, he said, was for someone to listen to him. Someone who would let him bare his ugly sores that perhaps would permit some kind of healing.

And he had this feeling, he said, that it ought to be someone from God's staff. So they could remind him of such things as perspectives and true values and hanging on to faith when doubting has become a way of life.

Sure, he was confident of his own ability to finally work his way out of his own difficulties. But only up to a certain point. Looking then at his hungry children, he began wanting all the help that he could manage. Just like the rest of us.

Wanting help from the Lord. From his friends and others. And from himself.

It takes some wisdom to accept that our best chances for doing and being what is needed in our lives are not entirely up to us. To our abilities and our efforts.

And I'm now more convinced it takes a special kind of man, with a special kind of inner resolve and courage, to look another in the eyes.

And say, "I'm scared. Where do I get help?"

Lord, let us understand that
we have your blessing to fail. And
to succeed.

# CRUTCHES

It is a rare moment. Filled with a special excitement that races through the mind and hurries on, infecting the heart.

People of widely differing backgrounds, but all sharing a common cause, are locked in heavy discussion. Of the Bible and what it means, or doesn't. Of God, and what he is or isn't. Of relationships. Getting down to the nitty-gritty of the whole business of being.

My friend, a smallish man with the expressive face of an Old Testament prophet, is leading the discussion. Perched on top of a table, he's the center of attention. Others have opinions and positions and are being heard with some attention and some respect. But when he speaks.

Everyone leans forward. Everyone listens.

Moving into those areas where we all live and have our realities, the talk had shifted to drugs and alcohol.

One member of the group, an adamant hostility lacing his words, delivered a pronouncement. An absolute from which, he made plain, there could be no possible exceptions. Nay, not even one.

There is positively no excuse, he profounded, for anyone to need crutches in order to get along in this world. It doesn't matter, he declared, whatever the problem, crutches are not the answer. And drugs and alcohol and anything that makes you dependent, he explained, are nothing but crutches.

My friend, certainly not unaware of the contempt in that high-and-mighty declaration, shifted around a bit. Took both his hands and moved one of his useless legs. Then reached over and picked up one of the metal crutches that enables him to walk. To be mobile. To be dependent, but not helpless.

Hey, he laughed, don't knock them until you've tried them!

With that small gesture, he reminded me that crutches, the right kind, are positive. They are contributing factors to useful and effective living.

As you can surmise, I've done some thinking about the incident. About that small slice of my life.

One thing that keeps itching me is understanding that having to use crutches does not mean the end of the world. Or of happiness. Or usefulness. Reaching that conclusion, for me, is closely related to learning there's nothing wrong with a man crying. When he hurts. And when his insides are being chewed on by his emotions.

That's quite a learning. It certainly is.

Especially when you've been taught from the cradle that it is a sign of weakness to depend on anyone or anything. When your earliest creed is the survival of the fittest. And your daily litany is a quest for total and absolute independence. To become the most autonomous in all autonomy!

That's not to argue that crutches of all sorts have not always been a part of my living.

It's just to be amazed and renewed by the fresh realization.

That my dependencies. On you. On my concordance. On my bifocals.

That my dependence on those crutches take nothing away from my wholeness. That, in truth, they even add some cubits to my stature. For indeed, they help me to be more what God intended me to be.

I'm saying a little prayer for my crutches.

Especially you.

# PLAIN NO GOOD

Her bitterness is mirrored by the tears filling her eyes. As she is talking, her hands are moving nervously from her lap to her face and back again.

It is my first meeting with Dorothy and I have been listening patiently to her story. Listening and hurting. Silently and prayerfully.

A lot of her talk concerns her children. Five in all. Only one old enough to be in school. Her mother's love caresses them gently even in speaking their names. Hearing that love is a joy. And an agony.

Her husband? Well, he's just about the closest thing to a saint the world is ever going to know. He's just wonderful. Faithful and forgiving. Honest and understanding. A man willing to work at two full-time jobs to maintain his family. I sensed her pride, the pride of a woman who knows the love of a man.

All of this, she explains, and I've done it again.

I tell you, I'm just no good. Just plain no good!

Slowly, between the hiccups and the tears, Dorothy lays bare the torturing truth. She is a compulsive thief. With a strange, psychological need to be caught and punished. And she has been. Again and again and again.

Sitting in the chapel of the county jail, where she faces a six-month term for shoplifting, she tells me the story.

It's not as sordid as it is senselessly tragic. Started at age sixteen when she became the mother of an illegitimate child. Her father is a good, God-fearing man and it was his response that set the stage for her life.

You see, he claimed her guilt as his own. Choosing to be a martyr, he left her crying out to be punished. And never understanding this strange need to have her father blame her, or beat her, or something. Anything except ignore her. As he had been doing for years.

That was our beginning.

In the weeks that followed, she began asking all sorts of questions. About loving and being loved. About God accepting us and what this means about our accepting ourselves.

I can't say that I know when it started. But one day I saw the blooming of a miracle. It was marked by an inner glow that gave Dorothy a most unique beauty. Seeming to bubble up from an unknown source, the miracle caught us both by surprise.

The miracle?

Dorothy began to believe in her importance as a person, as a wife, as a mother. She began to take seriously what she had been hearing all of her life. That God loves her. As this truth shattered the shell of defeat in which she had long lived, it was a beautiful sight.

Well, that was more than three years ago.

Dorothy served out her jail sentence and went back home. Returning to a loving and trusting husband. To children who welcomed her with excitement and celebration.

She went back into the free world, she said, afraid. Afraid of being tempted and not being able to resist the temptation. Afraid of losing what she had found. Afraid that she would let us all down. Me and God and her family and herself.

Yet, she told me, she also went with confidence. Fiercely hanging on to the lifeline looped around her heart. Knowing that she is special. To God. To her family. To me. To herself.

Just the other day I received a telephone call. One of the kind that many of us hate to get. And it was on account of Dorothy.

The caller said it was important.

Would it be possible, I was asked, would it be possible for you to be the speaker for our next program?

Oh, the caller went on, did I mention that Dorothy suggested you. She's the new president of our Parent-Teacher Association. A fine woman. The first black woman we've ever elected president.

I'll be there. Yes, ma'am, I'll be there.

꙰꙰꙰꙰

Lord, make us so conscious of the
miracle of your love in our lives that we
will recognize and accept that same miracle
wherever it happens. And however.

# LAST CALL

There's something about a telephone ringing in the middle of the night that does something to me. Right off the bat, it causes me to sit straight up in bed. Next, it sets off a chain of negative emotions and I always have this feeling of instant disaster. Finally, it usually provides enough motive for me to pick up the receiver and say, Hello.

Sometimes it is a wrong number. And I appreciate that. I really do. When my telephone rings after midnight and the only message I get is that some idiot wants to talk to Gladys and dialed my number by mistake, you'd better believe that I am happy about it.

More often it is not a wrong number. It's somebody with news that isn't good, or it is someone who has a friend or a spouse or a child who needs help. Or it is someone who wants to talk about living and dying, and it is most often someone crying for help.

That's the way it was the night Jacob called. Except that I was still awake. Studying the new car advertisements in the evening paper. Doing what my wife calls foolish dreaming. But what's so wrong about that?

Anyhow, I recall vividly the irritation that literally swept over me when I recognized the whining voice on the other end of that telephone line. It was a voice that I had come to know well since first hearing it in the county jail hospital some six months earlier. It was the voice of a man who was constantly carping about the cruel world. Who complained bitterly and regularly and loudly that all of life is nothing but a joke. And God is the worst joke of all.

Jacob had been born a Jew some sixty years before in a small town where Jews and black people, he claimed, were treated about the same. By the time I had come to know him, he disclaimed any real relationship with God. Or man.

Through the years, he had become a drug addict. And a con artist. Probably a lot of other things. Three different times he had served sentences in the state penitentiary. Always for things that he didn't do. Because some people had it in for him.

When I met him, in the hospital ward of the jail, he was just recovering from a close call. He had saturated his system with a narcotic by drinking several bottles of cough syrup. He was having a rough time, his whole system was in a state of rebellion, and his nerves were as tender as a pound of ground round.

In the weeks that followed, Jacob learned that I would listen and he began risking himself with me. A little bit at a time and then a little more.

So, when it seemed that he was maybe as normal as he would ever be, I was able to get him released. And found him a place to stay where he would be treated as a person with a drug problem. Not as a drug addict.

Remembering, I can say that he was cautiously grateful. Not really all that sure of my friendship. Quite leery of everyone else. Still, the days and the weeks came and went, and it seemed that he was making some progress. All of us who were concerned began relaxing.

Then he simply went back to his old habit.

And became a pain in the neck to everyone and anyone who had ever been involved in helping him. Months went by and it was always the same when I heard from Jacob. Nobody really cared about him. Nobody would really do anything to help him. It was always the same. Whenever he called, it was because somebody had kicked him out, without cause. He was a Jew. He would take no more. So he had to get out.

Hearing Jacob's nasal twang then was not all that surprising. His words were blurred enough for me to know that he was on some kind of high. A shudder went through me. Like the voice itself was clawing at my soul.

I'm down at the bus station, he said, and I'm getting ready to leave town. All I need is just enough money to get me down the road apiece. I've got a job waiting for me there. Listen, if you'll just bring me enough money to buy the ticket, it's only $11.40, if you'll do that, I'll get out of your hair. You won't have to worry with me again.

Jacob, darn it, what kind of a fool do you take me for? As often as I've come running when you've called. As often as you've agreed that kicking your habit is your first priority. Now you get yourself high, run out of ready money to keep it going, and call me. No more, man. Not me, Jacob, not me!

You're just like all the rest, he said. You don't care either.

To ease my conscience, I guess, I did telephone his brother. Oh, yes, he had some family. But they had long ago been worn out and used up by his spongelike need for help.

The brother was cordial. As cordial as most anyone could be when awakened in the early morning to hear that a prodigal brother was outside the camp. Calling for help. He was cordial, and indignant. Said Jacob had devoted his life to breaking promises, draining hope from his family.

Well, I didn't feel quite that bad anymore. About saying no to Jacob. After all, his own brother agreed that it was futile and hopeless to go on helping someone who refused to be helped.

I never heard from Jacob again.
But I did hear from the brother.
He called me three days later.
Said he thought I'd like to know.
They found Jacob. Dead. From an overdose of drugs.

Oh, yes. The brother thought I would appreciate knowing that he had done right by Jacob. He'd paid for a very fine funeral.
With lots of expensive flowers.

Oh, God!

# RECESS

It happened in an old and run-down part of our town. Over where
most folks live in frame houses with peeling paint and sagging
porches propped up with broken bricks. Or they make-do in an
abandoned car. One of the hundreds that jam the vacant lots like
Cadillacs at the country club on Sunday morning.

I had been driving through the neighborhood for a long time, it
seemed, trying to find where I was going. Not that I was all that
lost, you understand. But maybe I had strayed a bit and had
become confused. Needing badly to get someplace and becoming
more frustrated by the minute.

Anyway, that's what I was doing. That's why I was where
I was, when I was. As a last resort, I pulled to the curb and
parked, grumbling to myself and conceding ungraciously that I
needed to unravel the map-reading mystery that had landed me
in this predicament.

Sitting there, stewing and steaming, I became aware I had
stopped at the back of a school. Looking across the expanse of
concrete stretching away from the storm fence that protects
passers-by, I saw the doors fly open and pre-teeners of all descriptions plunged out onto the playground in a mad and frenzied
dash toward man's eternal dream.

Freedom!

And why not? It was recess!

You understand my enthusiasm for that moment, don't you?
In excitement, I remembered recess had always been my favorite
subject. Probably still is. Despite the world's frowns and what such
an attitude does to the Protestant work ethic.

Besides, watching the ebb and the flow of children and their
games was a welcome escape from the frustrations of the moment.
Hearing the squeals of laughter and the screeching of little girls

playing tag rolled back the years. Tuning in to the banshee howls of little boys battling for "king of the hill" was a fresh passport down memory lane.

But time, dad-gum it, doesn't tarry.

It came now, elbowing me away from that scene, not letting me drink as deeply from the fountain of youth as my heart desired. Then, as I was leaving, it happened.

A tiny bit of a girl-child, pigtails strung out in the breeze, all broken out in giggles, came dancing and skylarking into the path of a boy. The kind that football coaches drool over. A tank.

The shock of the collision was brutal. She was sent crashing, sliding, and skinning across the pavement. A long breath later, she sat up, screaming and crying as only a fearfully wounded nine-year-old can.

That ol' tank never slowed down. Nor looked back.

In less time than it's taking me to tell you this story, a teacher was there. At least she must have been the teacher, although her diminutive size and obvious youth suddenly made me aware that teachers are getting younger and prettier these days.

But she sure acted like a teacher. Striding quickly and purposefully toward the bawling child, she seemed both aware of and ignoring the clamor as a dozen small news reporters excitedly explained what had happened. All at the same time.

Reaching the victim, she examined her unhurriedly for obvious injuries. Finding only minor abrasions, she kneeled in front of the child, took her shoulders gently but firmly, and spoke in quiet, soothing tones. The screams gave way to sobs and sniffles. The eyes that had been squeezed shut in fear and hurt opened just enough to peek at that loving, familiar face.

Then two little arms wrapped themselves gratefully around a most receptive young neck, and that tear-streaked face was quickly buried in the soft warmness of an inviting shoulder.

How do you describe it?

Spontaneous and mutual love? The age-old protection and trust feelings of mother and child?

Choose your own words. There's still nothing else quite like it in this world.

I wanted to laugh aloud. Instead I found myself blinking away unexpected tears.

It was only much later. When I set out to share this story with you that I remembered.

The young teacher is white. The little child is black.
As if that mattered.
As if that ever mattered.

# POTPOURRI

Have you ever poured a few drops of water into a hot skillet? Testing, maybe, to see if it is hot enough to cook your pancakes? Remember how they bounce around, almost frantic to escape the searing heat? And, finally how they just sizzle away?

Well, sometimes that's the way my thinking is. Ideas and thoughts bumping into each other seeking to be expressed. Often fizzling away when they are kept closed up.

I'm learning, ever so slowly, to let them out. Whenever and however. And no matter. Hope that's OK with you.

One thing.

Playing tennis the other morning while the sun was starting to look over my shoulder, I pulled a hamstring. Well, what I did was to get a little bit of a strain in a muscle back of my thigh, but the other sounds more impressive and athletic.

Since then, as the sports announcers say, I've been "playing hurt." I grit my teeth and try to ignore the pain. And I limp a lot to try and get sympathy from opponents and spectators alike.

In the midst of a recent match, it dawned on me that I wasn't playing very good tennis. Pulled muscle or no pulled muscle.

But I was talking a lot. You know. Little friendly remarks that are intended to disconcert your opponent. Some people call it "needling." Others refer to it as gamesmanship.

Whatever name you give it, it is trying to win without being the better player. It's an effort to cover up your shortcomings with a lot of yak.

And right then I thought.

How often am I doing that same thing while making my way through life?

While kidding myself it doesn't really make that much difference? Well?

Another thing.

A Mexican man came by. Looking for a place to stay, he said. Just for tonight, *señor*. I have a job that starts *mañana*. Then I can pay.

I was too busy to really listen.

And, besides, the story sounds the same, in broken English or broken Spanish. And the odds are good that "a place to stay" still translates as a bottle of wine.

Anyway, I gave him a little money. Not much, but maybe enough.

But I didn't take the time to give him anything of me.

I wonder.

Jesus, was that you?

And still another.

He couldn't have been more than forty-two or forty-three years old. But he had lived a lot.

Almost from the beginning, they said, life had been hard for him. He had tried a lot of different things in an effort to measure up to life. Some of them good. Some bad.

Tragedy was his shadow. Their paths crossed from time to time. Until one day last week. Then the skirmishing was over and they came face to face.

With his father in the hospital and not expected to live, he telephoned his mother. He comforted her, said he would see her later, and closed a warm conversation with the assurance of his love.

Later he talked with his wife. Just about being a little late for supper. And the events of the day. How his dad was doing. Before he hung up, he told her he loved her.

That was all.

A few moments later, he killed himself.

Life is not deserved.
It is a gift.
To be cherished.
To be filled full.
To be treated for what it is. A miracle.
Celebrate the miracle.
Celebrate life.
Celebrate you.

# DOES GOD MAKE HOUSE CALLS?

It's late on a Saturday afternoon. One of those hot and humid days when dogs and cats share the same shade. Maybe unaware. Certainly uncaring.

The sun is still blazing relentlessly against the west wall of the smallish 12×24 frame building that is my study. I can tell you exactly how hot it is because that's where I am. Painting the clapboard siding in my best Tom Sawyer fashion.

Understand now, this is not something I do for amusement. Nor for therapy. Not even to relieve all those pressures that everyone else says I'm bound to have. I am painting because the little house badly needs it. And my neighbors have been making snide remarks about it. And because my wife has given me an ultimatum.

Anyhow, there I am.

Sweat streaming from every pore. Precariously perched atop an ancient and rickety stepladder, doggedly daubing paint on boards grown thirsty from long neglect. Wondering how I could manage to get myself a rejuvenating drink of something tall and cold without having to get off my wobbly perch.

About then, despite the clattering din of our air-conditioning compressor, I faintly hear the ringing of the telephone. Idly, I wonder what teen-ager is calling which teen-ager and how in the world was it possible that the telephone was not being used in the first place.

Breaking the reverie of the moment and destroying the rhythmic stroking of my painting, the raucous voice of my youngest son screams from the back door. Dad! Telephone!

Suddenly a cold chill begins walking along my spine and a small knot is tightening in my stomach. A butterfly seems to be lightly brushing my innards as I climb slowly and reluctantly to the ground.

Which one of you, I wonder, and what has happened?

Fearfully, and with a momentary resentment for the intrusion, I take my time walking to the big house. Offering a silent prayer that the call be a casual one. That it might even be one of those overbearing telephone solicitors wanting to sell me a sewing machine. Or a magazine subscription. Almost anything. Except don't let it be a death call. Not today!

Stopping to towel the sweat from my face and arms, I wondered how many calls, through the years, have come on Saturday afternoons. I don't know, but it hasn't been as many as have come after midnight during the rest of the week. You see, there's just the one Saturday afternoon. Right?

Detouring through the kitchen to get that cold drink, I suddenly acknowledged how fortunate I am. How blessed. There are people who never receive telephone calls. At good times or bad.

There are lonely people all over this city who would give almost anything to hear the ringing of their phone. To feel once more a part of life. To have someone recognize that they are alive.

Thinking about this, I move to my own telephone with a lighter, more confident step.

Then.

Your voice, familiar in its agony, came out of the instrument. Came with a despairing question. Came and then was hushed, waiting for my answer.

"Does God make house calls?"

Well?
Does He?

# PIE IN THE SKY

Friend of mine the other night was reminiscing about ordering things from a catalogue when he was just starting to wear long britches.

We'd gotten off on the subject because the women in this discussion kept insisting on talking about shopping and spending money. You know how they are.

Anyhow, he still vividly remembers sending off for a steam engine. He spent a lot of time and thought deciding, and he was almost beside himself waiting for it to come.

Every day, he would get out the catalogue and go over every little detail. He still recalls how that engine works, how it was built, and all the things he could do with it.

Then the big day. His steam engine came by parcel post.

You're right.

There's no way the real thing could measure up to the dream. The most important difference, as he remembers it, was the size. It was less than half as big as he had been expecting. When he opened that package and saw his beloved steam engine, it was some kind of disappointment.

Man, I know the feeling. Do I ever!

During my senior year in high school, I joined a suit club.

There was a tailor's shop on my paper route and whenever I had a chance I would stop by and look at the pictures of the elegant suits. Each with a swatch of material to let you really see what the suit would look like.

Since I didn't own a suit, I wanted to get the best one possible. So I joined the club. Paid $2 a month for eighteen long months.

Long before I finished paying for it, I had decided on the suit I wanted. It had a single-button coat, a double-breasted vest, and it was a pin-stripe 100 per cent wool.

I wanted to surprise my parents and everybody. So the tailor and I kept it a secret.

At long last, I made the final payment. My friend the tailor brought it out. Made exactly the way it looked in the picture. From the same material that I had so carefully selected.

Want to share my feelings when I tried it on?

Shut your eyes and imagine a short, fat kid wearing a tight-fitting green pin-stripe suit with a double-breasted vest and you got the picture!

If steam engines and green suits were the only things involved, I wouldn't be getting this worked up. Believe me.

But you've had some experiences that didn't live up to their advance billing, haven't you? Or, like me, you've paid good money to go places and see sights that were less interesting and less entertaining than the come-on.

Even more distressing, and far more important, are those times when people are disappointing. When they are not as attractive, not as charming, not as forceful, not as intelligent, not as charismatic, just not as something. As I was expecting.

Maybe that's the clue. Expecting.

I am rarely disappointed with people I happen to meet. And my disappointment with others seldom lasts when I get to know them, if I'll let myself have that chance.

What sometimes happens is that I build you up in my expectations to such a point that disappointment is inevitable. You're just not able to live up to my romanticized version of how you ought to be!

Like ordering out of a catalogue, measuring you by my expectations, rather than accepting you the way you are, is most likely to be disappointing.

For both of us.

And vice versa.

P.S.

My friend says that once he got used to it he had a lot of fun with that steam engine.

The green suit?

Let's leave it with this. I did get a lot of wear out of it. I didn't have any choice.

# TRUSTING

Night thoughts.
Shared with a rowdy, blustering thunderstorm.
Tinged with pain.

The statement was actually only an off-handed remark. Meant to be a joke. Or was it?

Everything's just fine, you said, except for people. And I agreed. Saying that life and stuff would go along a lot smoother at our place of business if we could just eliminate our people business.

Now I'm kicking myself.

Oh, I know it was no big thing. Neither of us was serious. The conversation was casual. Most probably forgotten immediately by you and everybody else involved.

Except me.

What makes me keep replaying that memory tape is the frightening knowledge that there are times when my behavior mirrors that attitude.

There are times when I am long on passing judgment and short on having patience. When I am too bull-headed even to listen to your point of view. Much less to hear it. And, God forgive me, times when I am too blind even to know you, except as the enemy.

Listen, being afraid to trust you is not my idea of a neat way to live out my days on this earth. In fact, not even a single day of the precious time that God has given us. I've seen it too often. It's a lonely, humorless and joyless vigil that constantly looks for and is always expecting the worst of other people.

Some of you are grumbling to yourselves right now. I can just hear you muttering. That's all well and good unless you've been treated the way I have. You just don't know, preacher, what it's like to be hurt by somebody you counted on as a friend. If you did, you'd know that's when you learn to keep people at a distance. So they can't do it to you again!

Mebbe.

But I have this funny conviction. That the less we are willing to trust, the more likely we'll wind up *feeling* that somebody has done us wrong! Know what I mean?

But besides that.

Honestly, I would rather be trusting of you than not. No matter how you behave. No matter what you do to me that denies that trust. Trusting you permits me to be at peace with myself and with my understanding of what it means to respond to God's love.

Trusting you, trusting people, starts with me. With me being secure. With me knowing that God is trusting me. And knowing that I am worthy of his trust because he makes me worthy. He creates me good.

Now that may be too simplistic for some folk. Maybe for you. This understanding that the business of trusting people is so closely connected with our relationship with God.

Or it may be too idealistic.

You may not believe that it is suited for the wear and tear of everyday use in the busy market places of our lives. Judging by the headlines you would have a point. But looking at the history of man offers a different view.

I sure can't make you see it my way.

But I'm trusting you to let yourself think about it!

Lord, you reach out your hands to all
sorts of people. You open your arms to
children and beggars and thieves and
prostitutes. You stretch your body on
a Cross. For me. For your sake, then,
give me faith enough in you to love
and trust your people.
He's waiting.
To hear your amen.

# LONELINESS

She's still young and attractive. But tiny lines are creeping out from the curve of her cheeks and on down past the corners of her mouth. Dark clouds, slowly gathering in the hidden valleys of her emotions, are starting to hover behind her eyes.

Nights are the worst, she says.

Hours of tossing and tumbling, moments of fitful sleep, followed by nightmares that end in screaming terror. Long, empty hours that seem always filled with an unknown menace stalking through the dark. Clawing madly at the locked shutters and rattling the attic windows.

And, even so, the days are not all that much better.

Before I even get up in the mornings, she said, I'm already tired. Tired of waking up in an empty house. Tired of being by myself. Tired of eating tasteless meals. Tired of waiting for someone or something new and different and exciting to happen in my life.

Not just tired, she wails. Worn out! Wearied to the marrow of my bones by the drabs and the blahs that bounce me from one day to the next. From one lousy month to the next lousy month. From year to year to year. From nothingness to nothingness.

> Oh, God, she weeps, what I really am is dead!
> So why don't You let me stop breathing?
> Please?

It is not that he is all that old.

Like he says, it's just lately that he's started feeling that the years are catching up. That maybe he's not a spring chicken anymore.

Started feeling that way, he says, not long after his wife died.

And his children, long since married and moved away, started this little campaign. To get him to take it a little easier. Go ahead, they suggested, take early retirement. A lot of people are doing the same thing these days. Just think of all the neat things you'll be able to do, all the real fun you'll have, when you don't have to work all the time.

Like what?

Maybe you can tell me, he was asking. What are all these exciting interesting hobbies that I'll be wrapped up in when I stop working?

Are they activities that will make me forget my memories? Will they take the place of the people who have gone out of my life? If I spend the days sitting on a park bench watching pigeons eating bread crumbs, will that satisfy the longings of my heart? Will it bring new joy and happiness into my empty old house?

You tell me!

What am I supposed to do now that they tell me that I'm old and they show me that nobody much gives a care?

You tell me!

The plaintive wail of loneliness is an ancient melody.

Young and old, aching hearts have always been at one with souls alone and isolated.

Mountains of lost hopes have ever sent forth freshets of tears, feeding the flood waters of despair.

But where, I ask, is it written that this must always be so? Where does it say that I have to feel lost and forsaken because there are many who do feel these defeating emotions? What makes it a law that I must concede my living to sorrow and pain because others about me have been willing to make that concession?

Thanks to God, you and I are able to choose our own life styles.

The Good News races through the house of my being with joyous abandon, awaking me over and over again with loving shouts of approval. My rooms are never long vacant, filled instead to overflowing with loving and trusting and sharing. Tenants who have moved in because of my accepting.

Loneliness?

Not unless my fear of loving overcomes and destroys the fellowship of His love for me.

But what about you?

∽∽∽∽∽

Lord, let me keep the pathway to
my heart cleared that your love may
enter freely; and let the joy of your
loving spill over from me that others
may share.

# THE SEARCH

When first I saw him, he was sitting on the couch in the hall just outside my office. With only a casual glance, I dismissed him as being no different from the many others who come, day after day, and sit there. Waiting for someone to speak. Waiting to be helped. Wanting a handout. And a drink. Just one, to get rid of a hangover.

I was hurrying on by when I heard my name.

The man on the couch wants to speak with you, someone said. He asked for you by name.

Rather reluctantly, I turned and went back. You see, it was a Sunday morning and that's the day that I am particularly busy and I don't like being distracted. Especially when it's just—well, you know what I mean.

But I did go back.

How can I help you, I asked the stranger? Then for the first time, I looked at him and really saw him. His clothing was simple and worn, but it was clean. He was wearing sandals, no socks. Something in his face told me that I couldn't write him off as a "bum." Whatever that is.

His eyes were clear, a penetrating blue, showing no signs of the alcoholic haze that blurs the vision of many who come to see me. He gazed at me searchingly out of a rugged and almost-handsome face. A neatly trimmed mustache added both dignity and a little severity to his appearance.

Perhaps you can help me, I'm not sure, he said. I'm looking for an honest man. Tell me, pastor, are you an honest man?

A little startled and suddenly suspicious that I might be hearing the opening gambit in a game designed to capture my sympathy,

I stalled. Well, I don't know, I replied. Maybe you ought to tell me what you mean by honest.

Something of a tired and disappointed look slid behind his eyes, but he persisted. It's simple, he said, I'm trying to find an honest man. Are you an honest man?

Now let's stop right there for a minute or two.

Put yourself into my shoes.

It sort of gets to you, doesn't it? Being honest is a complicated and involved matter. There are all sorts of things to be considered.

Like when you come walking into the office and you've had a fuss with your wife and a bank note is a week past due and you're having a migraine and your boss looks up, smiles and says, Morning, how ya feeling?

Do you give him an honest answer? Taking a chance on starting a conversation that could snowball into total disaster? Or do you slide that phony smile into place and give it to him loud and clear. Fine, I'm just fine. And you?

And what about all the laws and ordinances that have a way of getting violated when you're in a hurry to make your hospital rounds? Or maybe even when you're rushing home to see the pro-football game on the tube?

See what I'm talking about?

Then to be questioned unexpectedly by a total stranger, no matter how remarkable, adds to the confusion. I found myself unable to give a quick, glib answer.

Weighing in my own heart the matter of my honesty, I decided that I was given to being as honest as my feelings will permit me in a life that is so demanding. With people, including me, who so often need compassion and understanding more than raw truth. Loving kindness more than honest frankness.

Yes, I said to the stranger. Yes, in my own way, I feel I am an honest man.

By this time, I knew that we were playing no game. This one who had come inside a house of God searching and seeking, had come with a purpose in mind. With a mission to fulfill.

Now a small smile creased his face and looking directly at me, he asked, Well, then, what word do you have for me?

There was a leap of excitement in the depth of my emotions. I swear it.

With no conscious thought that I am able to recall, I replied. Speaking softly but firmly and sharing the word that I knew he was seeking.

God loves you, my friend.

He smiled again. Murmured thanks. And walked out of the door and out of my life.

I'll always wonder a little.
Won't you?

# THAT FIRST JUMP

Men's words, no matter how brilliant, are mostly lost as quickly as a meteor that flares and streaks across the sky and fades into nothingness.

But there are some happenings, some vignettes of real life, that are never forgotten. Told and retold, they live in memory.

This happened one summer not long ago.

He edged cautiously toward the edge of the swimming pool. An inch at a time. Teeth chattering and body shivering despite the midday sun. In contrast to the browned and bouncing kids around him, he was wearing a cotton T-shirt to protect his pale skin. To keep it from burning, his nose was covered with a yucky-looking white grease. And on each side of that hideous blob, tears slowly slipped and slid past his mouth and on down his thin little face.

Treading water patiently, his swimming instructor was urging him to jump into the pool. The eight-foot-deep end of the pool. Much less patient, his fellow students shouted and jeered and called out all sorts of advice. None of it heard. None of it heeded. Passers-by stopped to watch the unfurling of this mini-drama.

That scene and all of its principals is stamped indelibly in my memory book of life's most winsome moments.

For the little boy, one hand stretching desperately toward his teacher and the other flailing the air behind him for something to hold onto, it was the ultimate moment of truth.

It was the showdown in OK Corral.

It was the split-instant before Hemingway's fabled bull came charging into the ring with death riding each wicked horn.

It was the eternity while watching the hand grenade floating through the air, and the slow-motion agony of seeing it roll toward my foxhole.

For that little boy, it had to be fear. Raw, gripping fear. The kind that brings bitter fluids surging up through your throat. That freezes your muscles and paralyzes your mind. Unreasonable. Illogical. Inescapable.

For the teacher, her pretty young face mahoganized by the routine of her days, it was an important challenge. A test that had to be passed. A measuring of her patience, her skill, and her understanding love.

It would have been so easy for her to give up. Petulantly, in the manner of frustrated parents, to order him to step to one side. To get out of the way so some "real" boys could show their bravery. It would have been so easy. To add more shame to what he already owned. To what already owned him.

Instead, she spoke quietly, persuasively, gently. For more than ten minutes she swam in place, holding her hands out to him. Letting him know she was there. That she would guard him against those unknown dangers in the water.

Slowly, painfully, he edged closer to the water. His face mirroring doubt and indecision and fear, he crouched to make his leap. Silently, I was praying for him to jump. For him to trust. I really prayed.

Suddenly he straightened and hurriedly backed away.

Can it be?

Is it so?

That man creeps about in this universe. Racked and ridden by his fears of the unknown. Fearful of risking. Of stretching his living. Settling instead for less than he is. Content with existing. Afraid of living.

All the while, patiently God's hand is stretched out, beckoning. Offering life to those who will trust. And leap.

What is it called?

Faith.

Back at the pool, the shivering youngster squinched his eyes together and with a final grimace literally hurled himself into the water. Came up choking and sputtering, paddled wildly for a few feet, grabbed his teacher and hung on for dear life.

But he had done it.
And so had she.

God and that swimming teacher knew all along what the little
boy and I are destined to spend our lives learning and relearning.

That first jump is the one that has to come before all the rest,
but it is never the last leap of faith in our lives.

It may not even be the hardest.

But it is the first.

# FAMILIAR CLUTTER

A brilliant blue sky is spread boldly across the horizon. Saucy little clouds are in a heavenly game of chase. Nippy breezes are curling around the corners of the house. And all that gorgeous sunshine is out in full force bringing warmth to old bones.

Adding a benediction to a sparkling jewel of a day.

This was the setting as I made my decision. Once and for all. No reservations. No looking back.

I decided to clean out the garage.

With a measure of self-discipline developed in a less permissive age, nurtured in that nationally known college of Hard Knocks, and perfected in the peak traffic hours of an ill-designed expressway, I set about the task.

Well, not right away, of course. First, there was the planning.

You can't just barge ahead on a job like that by physically doing something. That would probably be disastrous.

You plan it out. Step by step. That way you save a lot of energy and you get through a lot quicker. In fact, I've been known to do such a good job of planning that by the time I had finished there wasn't any need to do it. That's what I call saving time and energy.

Contemplating the clutter of that garage convinced me that I wasn't facing an easy assignment.

Mounds of old newspapers and magazines spill across a broken-legged Ping-pong table. An upside down bicycle frame waits expectantly for the return of long-gone wheels. An abandoned croquet set, balls weathered and cracked, sits forlornly beside a new and never opened do-it-yourself antique paint kit. Like yesterday's ideas confronting tomorrow's youth.

Having contemplated for what seemed to me to be a proper time,

I pulled up a yard chair to do some strenuous thinking. Somehow, with my advancing years, the powers of my concentration are greatly increased when I assume the proper, sitting-down, meditative position.

My first thought was to holler for my wife.

You see, there's this old barrel sitting over in a corner. Right next to the cast-iron cooking stove that has a life-time guarantee and which I'm hanging on to in order to find out about the guarantee.

What I had in mind was getting her to shove that barrel over close to where I was sitting so that I could properly inspect the contents. However, remembering her nose was still out of joint from earlier when I was supervising her house cleaning (all I did was point out a few little cobwebs that have been around since last spring), I had a second thought.

Forget the barrel and work on the shelves.

With real determination, I scrunched my chair over and began sorting through the odds and ends congregating in the midst of last year's grime and this year's dirt. The useless things, I thought, I'll throw away. Stuff that is still serviceable, I'll keep.

Like the bicycle baskets. Boy, those can really be handy to have around. I've got eight altogether. They'll be just perfect for hanging on the garage wall and using as storage bins. Well, even if I don't do that, they are sort of decorative. Sitting there, year after year, giving birth to a new one with the replacement of each bike.

And that ol' combination can opener and bottle-cap remover. What does it matter if both ends are solid rust? If we have a power failure, you can bet we'll come looking for it.

To say nothing, absolutely nothing, about that hundred-foot garden hose that was left out in the freeze two winters ago, or was it three, and now has more holes in it than the church's budget. Really. Any day now I could need a six-inch piece of hose for something or other. Why get caught short?

With the sun sinking behind the roof and those nippy breezes beginning to cultivate a fresh crop of goose bumps and the meditative posture doing nothing to help old, cold bones, I didn't have any trouble deciding that I had labored long enough and hard enough. For one day, anyway.

Before leaving, though, I looked around with great affection at the familiar clutter of my garage. And I was happy as could be. I know that there is yet a task for me to do. Someday.

Lord, in the midst of my funning, get serious with me. Don't let me put off any longer cleaning out the garage of my living. Make me smart enough to keep what's good, in your sight, and strong enough to get rid of that which is useless, that causes the cluttering of my heart.

# WRINKLES OF FEAR

It was just a thirty-five-minute flight and I had this book I wanted to start reading and a personal problem or two that I needed to be thinking about. So it seemed smart, and practical, not to get involved with the man sitting about two inches from me.

Besides, he was looking out of the window and paying no attention to me. And how would I feel if I spoke first and he didn't answer? If he went on ignoring me?

Just when I finished buckling my seat belt and was hunting my place in the book, he turned away from the window and looked at me. Maybe it was my imagination, but there seemed a sort of unspoken, hopeful expression in his lined face.

Hi, I started it off.

After we had exchanged names and a few pleasantries, it all came pouring out. Like flood waters spilling over a dam. Like rocks sliding down the side of a mountain, gathering momentum as they go.

He began telling me all about himself. His business. He owns a small, successful company that is making more money than he ever dreamed possible. His children. A fifteen-year-old daughter who has him baffled and a ten-year-old son who is the gleam in his eye, the lilt in his heart.

And, then his wife. It's not a very unusual story. They were married early, before either one had time to ripen. Like a watermelon that is picked while it is still green, the marriage simply failed to develop. On the outside it looks OK. Inside, there's bitterness and disappointment.

I don't believe I could have stopped him from talking about it. The pressure was too great. He had to let it out. And I was safe. I was a total stranger and there was no risk in the sharing. No threat in the revealing.

He had been thinking and brooding for a long time. About another woman. About divorce. About suicide. About the dreariness of his now, the emptiness of his tomorrow.

I listened.

And I grieved. Not so much for the mess that had been made. Perhaps not even enough for the lives that are being warped by the circumstances.

But, mostly, I grieved for those strange barriers that keep us from trusting in life. That bar us from the honest sharing that feeds our emotional health. That nurtures our happiness and well-being.

I grieved for the timidity of man that keeps him eternally shackled by fear of rejection. That induces him to wear strange masks in relating to those he loves and lets him spread his heart before a passing stranger.

I grieved. And I listened.

It was a brief thirty-five minutes. Too soon swept away.

As the plane was landing he was apologizing and saying, Somehow, I feel better. You really have helped me a lot.

But had I? Had my willingness to serve as a sponge for the outpouring of his aching heart—had that really helped?

Or did his unloading on me just postpone that inevitable moment when he will no longer be able to hide his inner feelings? When he will have to take the ultimate risk?

Of being alive.

To himself and to his wife.

To God.

And to love.

Whatever that means for him.

⁊⁊⁊⁊⁊

Lord, let the touch of your love vanish the wrinkles
of our fear. Let the confidence of our trust in you flush
us from our hiding places. Let us come to know, in you,
honesty of life, and love.

# LOGS AND SPECKS

Man being a social animal and all, the conversation in our small group was drifting hither and yon. As so often happens. It was also deteriorating somewhat.

Well, to be honest about it, it was starting to sound like a pack of hounds baying after an ol' coon in a Mississippi River swamp bottom. Get the picture?

Just about the time that the gossip would start getting close to the jugular, there would be a distraction of some sort and the pack would go galloping off onto another trail.

OK. Maybe I'm exaggerating a little bit and it wasn't really all that bad. It sure did seem bad. Suffocatingly bad.

Finally, one of the group spoke up and in a gentle voice asked, Isn't there something in the Bible about getting the log out of your own eye before you try to remove the speck from your brother's eye?

There was a brief, incredulous moment of silence.

Then the leader of the pack fired back. There sure is, he barked, and that's exactly what I am talking about. This guy has been the log in my eye long enough, I'm gonna get rid of him.

Now, maybe he was funning me, pulling my leg. I don't know for sure and it is unlikely I will ever find out. But that's not what is important right now.

That whole incident has started me thinking about the matter of criticizing other people. Of sitting in judgment on their behavior and their ideas and their attitudes. Of trying to have them all fitted into the boxes that are in keeping with my views and my values and my approach to life.

One thought keeps bobbing up.

That sort of carping criticism, so often the result of professional jealousy or marital friction or personal frustrations, is a loser's game. Even when I am convinced that my intentions are good, it is still a lose-lose situation.

When I'm poking around with my rather blunt forefinger, and my out-dated parent tapes, trying to get the speck out of your eye, two things are happening.

You are being made to feel something is wrong with you as a person. That you don't measure up. That you've been judged and found guilty.

And I'm not taking care of my own shortcomings. I'm using you as an excuse not to deal with those behavioral problems blocking my vision of life.

Maybe.

Maybe if I would take seriously the idea that you are a brother. A sister. That you and I are bound in a family relationship declaring we are joint heirs of a singular grace.

The grace of life.

Maybe if I could live this part of my believing, I could learn to be less judgmental. Of what you do. Of how you look and what you say. Even, God help me, even less judgmental of what you believe!

I'm going to try it. Honest. I am.

Every time I hear myself saying about someone who's not present, Well, he's a nice person, but . . .

Every time I catch myself getting ready to insist that you ought to change your political views, your social consciousness, your theology, your . . .

Every time I have this strong feeling that our relationship would be beautiful if you would shape up and get in step with me . . .

I'm going to ask the Lord to nudge me. Just a little, you understand.

Enough to remind me to concentrate on my log and to give you my loving support while you take care of your speck.

When you get right down to it. Even if I didn't have my own log to think about, I still could not remove your speck.

That's something you will do, or not do.

As you choose.

By His grace.

# BOGGLED MINDS

Obviously using all the forbearance he could muster and then some, one of my teen-agers was patiently describing the extent of the universe to me.

As he was talking, in a matter-of-fact manner, of millions of light years and scientific theses of distance and time, I could only sit there with my amazement hanging out.

Before I put down in writing what I think he was telling me, a couple of things need to be plainly stated. Scientific, I'm not. I never cease to be amazed by whatever magic it is that makes the telephone work, and television is totally beyond my comprehension.

In the second place, I am absolutely not responsible for accuracy in reporting what I thought I heard and neither do I vouch for the truth of his statements. Understood?

If you want to get right down to the nitty-gritty of the whole matter, the things he was saying so boggled my mind that I no longer trust my memory. And don't ask why I didn't consult the Public Library or somebody to check him out. That would have been too simple. Besides, if it turns out that he's a fraction or so off, it still won't make that much difference in my life. Or yours.

Tack on to that defensive bit of reasoning the fact that it is the sweep of the concept that is so overwhelming. So mind blowing.

In our discussion, he was pointing out that our world is only a tiny part of a small galaxy situated near the outer edge of the universe. And this universe, he calmly contends, is made up of millions of millions of galaxies, and nearly all of them are larger than the one we're such a small part of.

Illustrating the immensity of the universe, he set forth the following hypothetical situation. At least, this is what I think he was saying.

If we could send a spaceship from our planet to the exact center of the universe, and it then made a U-turn (provided such is legal there) and returned to land safely on earth, a couple of significant things would have happened, he said.

In the first, according to his calculations, the occupants of the spaceship would have aged about ten years while making the journey. That's not all that bad, I ventured. I spent longer than that trying to teach your mother how to parallel park.

Then he dropped the other shoe.

The earth itself, he declared, would then be 30,000 years older!

Isn't it strange how we can be so impatient?

How sometimes we cry out in fury and frustration because we don't grasp the mind of God?

And isn't it even more incredible?

That He continues to infect us with faith to know that He loves us and causes us to love each other and to love ourselves?

Boggled minds and all!

# SLIVER OF TRUTH

A loving father, anguish advertised in the tiny drops of sweat beading his upper lip, is painfully reciting his difficulties as a parent. Especially as the single parent of teen-agers. Single because long ago a young wife had become disenchanted with changing diapers and wiping runny noses. Had just walked off and left a note. Saying she wanted some time to live.

Mouth tightening and lower jaw jutting out to challenge any and all intruders, he keeps reciting one dominating refrain. Saying it over and over again. His litany of release. The assurance of his pardon.

All I'm trying to do, he explains in exasperation, all I'm trying to do is to keep my kids from making the kinds of mistakes that I made. I just want to straighten them out so they won't do the stupid things their mother did. It's a shame for them to have the same kinds of trouble that I was always having. And especially since I can keep them from it!

Then, oozing self-righteousness and a certain kind of defensiveness, he turned to his sobbing seventeen-year-old daughter and issued an absolute, an ultimatum: That's what my daddy did for me and, by God, that's what I'm gonna do for you!

> O Lord, what does it take for me to learn?
> What is it, God, that crinkles my love with the
> sour breath of fear? That withers my trust and
> breeds rank suspicion? And eats away my heart
> of understanding?

Protected by the ages, known to all the prophets, a razor sliver of truth slices through the tragedy of our smothering instincts.

It's a fact of living that emerged with screaming clarity about

the time that Adam and Eve took to messing around and got
everything all bollixed up. As you well know, that was a spell
ago.

That fact is this.

Nobody.

No child nor parent. No husband nor wife. No friend nor
stranger. No Greek nor Jew. No male nor female. No. Not one.

Nobody can be sheltered from experiencing their own existence.
Neither can they be protected from making their own mistakes.

Let's put it a different way. A positive way.

Each of us is permitted the agony and the ecstasy of becoming.
Of learning and growing. Of loving and living and losing.

Because a loving Creator is gifting me with the freedom of
choosing, there is a fierce and a wild joy in each decision. My decision. My own personal decision.

Right or wrong.

Mine.

⧟⧟⧟⧟

Jesus, Lord, so often I am blind
to this special need of those who
are nearest and dearest. Their need
to be. For me to let them be. To
let them become. Seize me, Jesus,
that my heart lights the way for
my mind.

# BALL BOY

I was thinking about doing a New Year's special. Something that would have tremendous intellectual impact and you could have it for ready reference. This was the way I was starting it out:

"Battered by our wars and our violence, even while buffered by our love and compassion, the old year creeps painfully out in the night to die. But without a whimper. With dignity and courage.

"Meanwhile, the newly born is welcomed wildly and raucously. Riotously celebrated as something inside us reaches frantically for the elusive hope of a new beginning. Desperately shaking the dust of old failures from our feet. And out of our lives."

With that brilliant opening, I was planning to move on to an examination of a few of the epochal world and national events of the year. Appraising and evaluating their historical significance. Always, of course, relating everything to the religious viewpoint. Naturally.

Just thinking about doing all that made me tired.

Thinking about having to read it afterward made me very sleepy.

Remembering, instead, some golden moments from here and there. The light touch of your hand in my time of distress. Some trusting conversations and reassuring smiles. The mingling of lives in the making of the workaday world exciting and vigorous.

Recalling times and places and people that have been joined to the parade of my happy memories, I'm claiming from you a special gift. For the starting of a New Year or a new day or a new life.

It is the sharing of this story.

The day is Saturday and the time is early morning. The place is a public tennis court. I'm playing with an old and loved friend, name of Bill or Willie or Hey, You.

Two small boys, about ten or eleven or somesuch, are watching. One of them, a talkative, live-wire type, is our volunteer ball boy. Hustling all over the place after straying tennis balls and tossing them back to us. Very helpful and very unusual.

The other one just stood there. First on one foot and then the other. Wanting, I felt sure, to be just as aggressive as the other youngster. Wanting to be a part of the activities. Wanting to be included. But just standing there.

> Oh, Jesus, Lord, how often have I stood on the side-
> lines and watched. Afraid to risk the offering of myself.
> Shying away from involvement with you and your chil-
> dren. For fear they might not want me. Or that I would
> not measure up to their standards. Or yours.

Like many a live wire, our helpful spectator burned brightly but briefly. A passing chum gave a yell, and off he went. To battle a dragon. Or play kick-the-can.

Bill and I were back to chasing down our own mistakes.

Until a ball rolled in the direction of the shy one. And he was asked to toss it back. Which he did, quickly and with great energy. Would you like, he was asked, to help us? By chasing our bad shots? Remember, there's more of them than otherwise?

You would have thought, seeing the sparkle in his eyes, that we had lassoed the moon and put him in charge of handing out slices of green cheese. He was that excited!

> Oh, Jesus, God, how many folk have I left out of my
> life? Because I wouldn't take just a moment to ask them
> in? How many lonely hearts have gone their lonely way,
> because I was too busy to ask them in to stay?

For the rest of our tennis game, Bill and I were treated like touring professionals. Our little friend, his name is Scott, was all over the place. Not only running his legs off chasing balls, but applauding our efforts. Which were limited, to say the least.

Visiting with Scott after we had run out of steam, I was impressed with his brightness. His zest for being. As I listened I was thinking.

> Lord, am I ever that willing to share myself with others? To spend myself doing for others? I wonder, Lord, if I still enjoy people and living and being that I can do something, anything, for the sheer joy of doing?

Maybe I won't ever see Scott again. Maybe I will. In either case, I cherish our time together. Not just for the lessons in Christ-living that were taught and learned.

But for the added dimension it gives to me.

For the part of Scott that will always be a part of me and of Bill. For the part of each of us that is now a part of Scott.

> Lord, keep me alert to beauty
> in every relationship. Teach me to enjoy
> and celebrate every moment of time that
> you have given me. And every person.
> Now.

# THE PRICE

There is a disturbing question that keeps bumping around inside of me. Demanding my attention. And getting it.

Most often it comes late in the evening, usually the last thing on my agenda before getting to sleep.

The things I did today?

Were they, in reality, worth the price that I paid for them?

Waking up in the morning I am caught up in a fresh excitement. A feeling of exultation that is in knowing that I am, and that I am a part of God's creation.

The wonder of my knowing brings a renewing of spirit. With smiling heart I gratefully acknowledge that God has given me this day. This new day.

It's all mine.

It's up to me how I use it. For good or for bad. For gain or for loss.

So the day moves along and things are happening. Decisions are made. Words are spoken and written. People come and go. Time keeps counting off. Never stopping. Never even the slightest pause. And it sweeps me along.

Crawling into bed to be refreshed for the next edition of God's gifting, I look back at my day. And, deep inside, I know the answer to that question.

Down deep, I know whether all I did and said and felt was worth the price I had to pay.

You see, I do pay a price. A big price.

And so do you.

The cost for me, and for you, is the same.
One precious day of life.

༄༅

O God, quicken me to seek full value
for each of my days.

# TRILOGY

## I

I was hungry, and you set up a
committee to discuss my hunger.

It's a sad old house.

The screen in the front door, barely hanging on to the frame, waves limply. Old tires and beer cans and rusting axles are just a part of the litter desecrating the front yard.

Inside is worse.

Chaotic clutter. Empty boxes stacked to the ceiling. Grimy furniture half-covered by dirty sheets and overflowing with odds and ends, with bric and brac, mostly broke.

The kitchen is revolting.

Greasy and food-smeared utensils stacked in the sink, on the counters and the rickety table. Covering the top of the stove and filling the oven. Unbelievable! Inside the refrigerator are pots and pans and dishes, each with a dab of dried, rotting food.

We were some shocked by the conditions. We shouldn't have been. Not all folks on welfare live in that kind of squalor. Probably not many of them.

But, then, not all folks on welfare are blind and living alone as this one. Existing may be a better word. Grubbing in her back yard to grow a few vegetables. Depending on the government for the rent money, waiting for the welfare to bring commodities.

Groping in the dark to stay alive.

We cleaned as best we could and we left the allotted staples. Rice, sugar, powdered milk, dried beans, some cheese and real butter.

And we visited awhile. Not long enough.

To feed her hunger that goes beyond hunger.

But she's only one. One of more than ten thousand in our community alone who are hungry and waiting.

# II

I was hungry and you felt sorry
for me . . . and felt sorry for me . . . and
felt sorry for me . . .

It's a funny little house.

Sort of leans to one side like a drunk trying to walk a straight line. Long ago, the clapboard siding had been yellow. Now it's more like hair that has been bleached and dyed much too often. With streaks of faded color mingling with patches of brittle gray. A mess.

The yard is empty and bare. Not even a weed surviving the erosion of time and indifference. A worn path sort of staggers toward some broken steps. A concrete block is serving as support where the sag of the porch comes closest to collapse.

Greeting our tentative approach was a swarming of brown-skinned, black-haired, dark-eyed youngsters. Bouncing with excitement. Bare feet puddling little dust clouds. Eagerness and anticipation overcoming shyness.

Mostly they were six, going on seven, and staggered under the heavy sacks of commodities that they insisted on lugging into the house.

Following them into their home, we were met by a smiling, patient-looking woman. While young, she looked old. Especially since her teeth have mostly rotted away. She's their mama. Also, she's head of the household.

Inside, the little house wasn't so funny.

Three tiny rooms, jammed with old furniture. But neat and clean. And oppressively hot. Everything seemed overflowing until we got to the kitchen and we discovered that it was empty. No food. Not one single item.

Looking into the faces of those children, I found myself trying to remember the last time I had really missed a meal. And what was it I recently read? About the amount of money we spend each year for weapons?

Before leaving, I wanted to find out from Mama what needs,

other than the obvious, were tugging at her life. Whenever I spoke to her, she smiled. But never replied. Finally one of the children told me what should have been obvious.

You see. I can't speak Mama's language. And it is extremely difficult for a poor, uneducated woman brought to this country and abandoned, it's most difficult for her to learn to speak mine.

The oldest youngster told me. She does what she can to survive. Her chief source of income is tending to the children of her neighbors. The ones who have jobs. And sometimes even the ones who don't.

Then she waits for the commodities.

For the welfare to come.

With all of its bounty.

## III

> I was hungry and you came by to
> tell me a meeting was planned . . . to
> decide if I was worthy of being fed.

It's a neat little house.

Imitation green shutters brightening the battleship gray asbestos siding. The front yard neatly raked and a row of half-buried pop bottles carefully guarding a freshly dug flower bed.

The porch was swept clean and there was no litter. Inside it was more of the same. Each of the three small rooms clean as the proverbial whistle. The worn old furniture comfortable and inviting.

Out back, a vegetable garden has been plowed and the rich black soil readied for planting. Amos, the man of the house, grinned from ear to ear when I marveled at all the work that he had been doing. Ducking his head, he shuffled back inside the house to show me the bathroom. His pride and joy.

Guess I was still bragging on the garden and Ida, his wife, heard me. Hah, she snorted, that ol' coot didn't do none of that. All Amos did was grin a little more when Ida explained that a neighbor came over every year to plow their garden.

It didn't take long to bring in the commodities and to put them away on the shelves. There was plenty of room.

But, looking back, I know that Ida and Amos were not all that interested in the food. Oh, it was welcome, all right. But they were more hungry for someone to talk to.

So we stayed awhile. With me trying my best to make a little sense from the ramblings of Amos, mostly having to do with those years when he worked for the railroad, if he ever did.

But much more interested in Ida's descriptions of her various husbands and their faults and their virtues. In hearing her cackle as she told how she had gotten rid of one after the other. Until Amos. And then feeling her pride as she told about all the children they had raised. Some theirs and some not.

I want to tell you something.

Those are extraordinary people. They are spry and vital and aware that God loves them and firm believers in His goodness being the only reason that people love each other.

They are not afraid of the arrows that fly by day nor of the terrors that stalk the night. The pestilence of despair has no place in their lives.

They rise in the morning, Ida and Amos, their ninety-year-old bodies once more renewed by the night's rest. They greet each new day with their wrinkled blackness creased by the smile of His love.

But still they hunger.

For your love. And mine.

# EASTER

Gray and dreary, the day is depressing. I can actually feel my spirits drooping and my enthusiasm smothering in the thick glumness of the weather.

Then the rain stops, suddenly and unexpectedly. Not according to predictions. The clouds are shoved aside by impertinent breezes. The sun peeks in, ducks away, then comes shining through and the day starts to sparkle. Nerves vibrating, the message is clear. It's good to be alive.

That is Easter.

In one corner of the room, paying no mind to the strange adults hovering around him, a little boy is squatting and squalling. Alternating between wails of despair and sobs of distress. Fighting off all attempts by the strangers to comfort him.

In the middle of his trauma, his mother returns. Coming through the door with her arms reaching out for him and a loving smile on her familiar and beloved face. Running across the room, he buries his face against her lap and his little heart gradually slows its wild beating.

That is Easter.

I've just come from the hospital and a tumor of grief is growing within me.

My friend is dead. Only yesterday he had been talking of going home. Where there had been so much hope and determination, now there is nothing. Death has ended everything.

Until I remember. As I was standing beside his bed that last time, he looked up at me, smiling. Don't forget, he said, I'll always be with you. In your memory. That's living, too.

That's Easter.

Tiredness gathering at the corners of my eyes and crawling along the laugh lines leading to my temples was interrupted by my sound of sounds. The ringing of a telephone.

What are you doing? Why aren't you home? Tried to get you there and they said you'd be late.

At first, the voice was only vaguely familiar. Then, with an explosion of feeling, I recognized it. A cousin, but more like a brother. From a long way off and a long time ago.

I'm at the airport, he said. Have an hour between flights.

It wasn't all that much, but it was something. It was seeing again. Touching again. Hurriedly swapping family data. Then, with tears stinging my eyes, watching him out of sight.

That, too, is Easter.

Wherever love lights and lightens my life. And yours.

Wherever there is some new beginning. A renewing of meanings. A flush of new hope in the midst of old hurts and old failures.

That's Easter.

Whenever there's a balm for the wounds of my spirit. A salve for those cuts and gashes that are mostly self-inflicted. A healing lotion for the betrayal of the Judas in me, for the denials of the Peter in me, for my desertions in the face of public pressure.

That's Easter.

Ah, now I see it.
What I do is let myself be free.
Free to be captive to the love of God.
In Jesus the Christ.
That makes Easter possible.
For me.
In all my living. And dying.
And living again.

# WHAT IS MAN?

By virtue and by vice, certain epochal events are permanently spread across the minutes of a man's life.

Often asking for, even demanding, retrospection.

One is a hot sweaty night in the long ago.

Somewhere off an island in the Pacific, dogged by enemy submarines and deviled by worn-out engine bearings, an overcrowded troop carrier rocks and rolls. Wallowing in her own misery.

Hunkered on the steel-plated deck of the tawdry old sea slattern are hundreds of grim-faced Marines.

Waiting fearfully for the whatever. Hoping faintly for the not likely. But resigned. Always resigned to the awful harshness of the real.

Shutting out the cloak of whispered curses that men wear to hide their honest emotions when facing danger and death, I looked out across the tossing sea. Empty and void of life, it seemed, and stretching all the way to eternity.

Then, in quick and unplanned desperation, I lifted my eyes to the heavens. Scanning the vastness of the universe, my shrinking soul cried out in prayer, O God, what is man?

Another is a crisp vacation morning in the Rocky Mountains not too long ago.

We had started down in the canyon, following the twisting trail of the Big Thompson River rushing tirelessly in the other direction to deliver its precious life-giving cargo.

Intimidated by the massive rock walls that sometimes tower thirty stories high on both sides of the road through the Narrows, I drove cautiously up and out of the valley.

Finally, after passing through the range of protective foothills,

we began the skinny, winding climb that would take us up, up
and away. Beyond the snow line. To a point almost three miles
above sea level. To a craggy peak stretching 15,000 feet toward
the heavens.

Stopping once or twice just for a taste of what it was like and
what it was going to be, that helped.

But I still wasn't ready. Not for that breath-taking artistry of
God's panorama. Not for such a close-at-hand, sweeping view of
mountains poking their beaks into nosy clouds. And angel tears
spilling in rivulets and then flowing out to feed the thirsty plains.

Throat filled with wonder at the magnificence of his design and
heart throbbing from the pleasure of his revelation, I heard a cry
going out from my soul, past those lofty peaks, O God, what is
man?

If perhaps you also have shared such moments when, with the
suddenness of a sharp gusting wind, you've been overtaken by
your own finiteness. And by the infinity of your Creator.

If you've ever walked your mind through a billion years and
then placed the work of your hands, the sweat of your brow,
alongside. In contrast.

Then you know my feeling.

You know my longing cry. My prayer.

And I hope you share the rest.

So God created man in his own image . . . male and female
he created them. God blessed them . . .

Yet thou hast made him little less than God . . . hast
given him dominion . . . hast put all things under his feet.

What is man?

God's finest work!

# TRAFFIC TICKET

A couple of hours earlier the morning had been fresh and zesty. Now it was settling down to business in a routine and determined way.

I was on my way back to the house for a quick shower and change of clothes after an exhilarating tennis match. When I win, the game is always exhilarating. When I lose, it's hard work and most likely a waste of time.

The last school bell had echoed through our town and only a few tardy scholars were still at liberty. Driving along the broad boulevard that intersects the street where I live, I was vaguely aware that there was little traffic. It was the lull between the time school starts and before the time that housewives begin their shopping forays. While they are having their second and third cups of coffee.

Less than a mile from my house, I drove along thinking about the tennis match. Then remembering the day and the work that it offered. Wondering if there were additions to the hospital list. About the tentatively scheduled meeting with a group from out of town. And a marriage counseling session that had been too long delayed.

There was nothing much unusual.

Except for one thing.

While one part of my mind was checking cross streets for traffic and another was ticking off the day's chores as they passed in review, there was a communication failure.

My eyes did not report to my brain two important sightings.

The first was one of those middle-of-the-street signs, painted a bright orange, that declares the area to be a school zone.

I have a rational answer for that. The nearest school is a high school that is exactly $7/10$ths of a mile away, on a totally different street. So, my eyes didn't believe what they saw and just refused to make a report.

The second sight that did not get registered was that of a blue and white automobile. With a red light mounted on its top. Parked on the street, directly under a sign that reads, 20 m.p.h., 7–9 A.M.

I first became aware of said vehicle when I glanced into the rear view mirror and saw it pull away from the curb with that red light flashing.

As you well know, by that time it was $49.50 too late.

That ain't cheap, you know. And I'm not all that convinced that it's fair, either.

Still, taking into account all the learning that goes along with the whole deal, it may not be too much to pay. The first lesson is the most obvious. Driving while thinking can be dangerous. And expensive.

And then there are the afterthoughts.

Like suddenly wondering how often I place my life and yours in jeopardy by being unaware of the warning signs along the way.

Like wondering if I'm living too fast and not even aware of it. Heading for a speeding ticket that demands of me a premature hearing before the judge of all life.

Like wondering if I can be so oblivious of the obvious, what does that say about my sensitivity to you. And your needs. To say nothing of others. Who may be less obvious but who have great needs.

And wondering when I will be mature enough to accept full responsibility for my mistakes. Without getting defensive.

If ever.

# SAINTS AND SINNERS

There is not a single thing new about this problem.

In fact, I've already called it to your attention. A couple of times.

But since it is something that I keep running right smack-dab into, chances are that you're just as lucky. Which is another way of saying it not only rains on us sinners, but it has been known to sprinkle on you saints.

The problem is communications.

Communications is right at the heart of how you and I get through this world.

Now you know I'm not talking about conversations. Even though they are important. And pleasant. Depending on whether they are dull or animated or whatever.

Probably, although not always, interesting and delightful conversations naturally grow out of learning to communicate.

Sometimes there are interminable conversations and absolutely no communication. And that's tragic. Couples just getting married always believe that they have "good" communications. Usually that means they enjoy talking about football and movies and television and the other people in their peer group.

Couples getting divorced, on the other hand, are just as positive that they have never had any sort of communication. What they say is, She never was willing to communicate, and, He couldn't even spell it, much less do it!

Parents argue that it is impossible to communicate with teenagers whose vocabulary consists of two-toned grunts spiced with an occasional "wow!" Teeners claim their nineteenth-century captors have a one-word vocabulary, "no." At least, that's what mine say.

But, you know, it really isn't funny.

Heartaches and heartbreaks by the millions live in all of us who suffer our relationships without real communication.

Still, I don't have an easy answer.

Just some hard advice.

Take a good look around you.

Look at where you are now, this day, in your many relationships. With your spouse. Your children. Your parents. Your business associates. Your friends. Anybody.

Now look at your willingness to share your feelings with those same people. Look at your willingness to trust yourself to them.

Maybe you would rather suffer your relationships than to share and trust.

It sure is a lot easier. A lot simpler.

But, oh God, it is so lonely!

# CELEBRATE THE RAINBOW

God said . . . "My bow I set in the
cloud, sign of the covenant between
myself and earth . . . between myself and you
and living things of every kind."
(Genesis 9:13, 15 New English Bible)

We are heading home.

A rowdy late-summer thunderstorm, jagged lightning and thunder crackling and popping in indignant litany, chases us through the mountains. Nerve ends jangling and tensed-up muscles rebelling from long hours of driving on those winding roads, we finally escape. Now, grumbling righteously, the winded storm hovers in the foothills. Awaiting new victims.

Greeting our race to safety with outstretched horizons is the comfortable and familiar prairie. Its rolling contour neatly halved by a shimmering ribbon of wet pavement zippering across the empty plains. After our ordeal, the stark emptiness of the land and the absence of violence are comforting.

Then.

Faintly at first, but growing in size and intensity until it is dominating the world.

A magnificent rainbow climbs out of the lushness of the land, arches royally across the gray sky and gently comes to rest again in a hidden valley.

Clouds, earlier chased and whipped by the angry storm, are being kissed tenderly by the brilliant colors. Their tears of happiness for this wound tending are a slight mist that freshens the day and cleans the air.

A welcoming that will long be remembered. And cherished.

Home. At last.

And rudely, suddenly, the bow in the clouds takes on a fresh reality. A deeper meaning is revealed.

For while we were adventuring and opening new vistas, being pleasured by our vacation and travel, day-to-day living had been going on. And day-to-day dying as well.

Only moments after returning, a telephone message drove me to my knees. In disbelief and grief. In shock and prayer.

During the past several years, four of us had shared a unique and a special kind of friendship. Including our joys and our sorrows, successes and failures, problems and opportunities. Our living and our loving.

None of us much alike. But all the same. Caught up in the same calling. To serve a Man and to share and make known His love to others. We played together and worked together. Griped about all the petty things that disturbed us separately and jointly. And shared both the heart-warming and the heart-chilling events of our lives. Public and private.

And now. The youngest one of our group is dead. Without warning. Like the lightning slicing through the rocky mountain. Like the bolt burning the bark from the giant spruce. That suddenly. That shockingly.

That happened awhile ago.

Where there was once a sharp and agonizing hurt that screamed in protest, demanding an explanation, now there is a dull ache. Sometimes seasoned by sudden, unexpected memories.

But there's more.

There's a growing trusting that comes with remembering. There's a special healing that walks hand in hand with trusting. And there's accepting that keeps pace with healing.

For God has made his message clear.

With a bow in the cloud.

With a son on a cross.

> O God, let the promise of your covenants
> soften the storm of my sorrow and end the
> deluge of my grief.
> Amen.

# THE LEAD TULIP

We went about twenty-five minutes early so we could be sure of getting decent seats. That was a good idea, except that a few hundred other people had a better idea. They arrived a couple of hours before we did and not only did they claim the better seats, they were also "holding" seats for late-arriving relatives and a few special friends who said that maybe they would come.

I would never have believed so many people would make a conscious decision to spend a beautiful Sunday afternoon in a jam-packed auditorium.

There was wall-to-wall humanity long before the first curtain call. Standees in the back and floor-sitters in the aisles. An excited and nervous crowd that periodically giggled in unison and was also prone to collective neck stretching trying to locate familiar faces.

I'm able to tell you all this with great accuracy because of the fine view I had. Seated on the last row, next to the aisle, downstairs.

By now, you have surely surmised that I was not in church. Not hardly. I was, however, in the midst of some of the Lord's chosen and in the company of a large number of people whose pride was more on display than their enthusiasm.

What I was doing was attending my granddaughter's ballet recital. And that's what all those other people were doing. Well, that is, we were all attending a ballet recital that featured more than four hundred and fifty ballerinas, ranging in age from three to eighteen. But I was there to see one ballerina. Know what I mean?

And why not? After all she is the lead Tulip!

That's right. The lead (rhymes with seed) Tulip. There were fifteen other Tulips and a Cheshire Cat on stage with her, but she was the lead. Her dark-haired beauty and her grace-filled movements were surely the focus of every eye in the place. Except possibly for a few jealous relatives of the other Tulips. And the Cheshire Cat.

I have to tell you that I was starting to get a little panicky before the Tulips made their entrance, welcomed by my resounding applause.

Maybe it was the close quarters and the large number of people.

Or it could have been my exposure to the Forget-Me-Nots, the Sweet Peas, the Daisies, the Butterflies, the Fireflies, the Dragonflies, and the Blue Bonnets. It seems to me that it would have been better staging if the Tulips had come on earlier—a lot earlier.

In all honesty, however, I do have to point out that they did precede the Butter Cups, the Rocking Horseflies (*the Rocking Horseflies?*), the Apple Blossoms and the Tiger Lilies.

It could even have been worse. A lot worse. For the Living Garden, in which the Tulips were led so beautifully by my talented granddaughter, appeared on the program just before the Mad-Hatter's Tea Party. And the Tea Party was before the action of the Queen's Court.

Being a considerate and thoughtful person, I vacated my seat in the auditorium while I was leading the bravos as the Tulips were leaving the stage. After all, there were people standing. And leaving when I did, after my granddaughter's starring performance, I missed only eighteen other groups. Imagine that, just eighteen. That's not too much of a sacrifice for an old sacrificer like me! Is it?

What came crawling across the nerve ends of my memory banks and what prompts me to share this little vignette are earlier days, other crowds in other places, and other children.

Remembering the excitement and the scared feeling. A feeling that something might mess things up for a son or a daughter.

I've been wondering a bit about the difference in anxiety levels. With my granddaughter the ballet star, I am supremely confident that everything is going to be perfect. With my daughter the ballet star, who was equally or more talented and grace-filled, I constantly was filled with dread. Expecting the worst.

I declare to you that there is something that God gives us in our maturity that is priceless. Paid for with age and experience. Perspective.

O Lord, season me with experiences,
temper me with challenges, but please
don't ever let me become complacent.

# A BETTER WAY

Mutual concerns.

That's what we were talking about. There were several of us sitting around, and that got to be the subject.

And what concerned us most, mutually and otherwise, was the how-to part of bringing about behavior change. That's presuming a whole bunch right there. Because that has to come after recognizing there is a need for change!

Inevitably, I guess, the discussion flowed over into the area of parent-child relationship. The whole matter of discipline and permissiveness. Sometimes I get a feeling that it's easier for us to talk about what's good for the children than to face up to what is needed in our lives. Huh?

Letting go of that for the time being, I have to say that our discussion was an honest questing for guidance. Even a hungry seeking for solutions to a relationship problem that's been around ever since that snake climbed a fence and slipped into the Garden.

I can't remember all the sharing. But there was a lot. Including some of the simplistic "chain of command" approaches that set my teeth on edge. Still, it was all out in the open and spoken from conviction. The sort of mutual concerning that does encourage growing and learning.

Yet.

Yet, I am still having some uneasy feelings. That I really didn't say what I wanted to say in the way I wanted to say it. You've felt frustrations like that, haven't you?

I wanted to tell you how I had spanked some of my children when they were small. Used a belt on older ones on rare occasions. And, at times, shouted and yelled to drive home a point.

But not because I was bigger and stronger, I told myself.

But in order to teach them, I believed.
To instill right habits in them, I was convinced.

Having done all that during the first fifteen to twenty years of parenting, I wanted to say, I have come now to recognize and to understand there is a better way.

It is founded on and rooted in what I know now of God's relationship with me. What I understand of his loving permissiveness in my life.

The way I believe our relationships are most effective and creative, with our children and with one another, is when they are based on the freedom that God gives us to make choices.

And then I wanted to add a little more.

This better way permits us to learn through living, and it even has room in it for our children to make some mistakes. And us, too.

A better way, for me, is one that is grounded on love.
And love cannot be beaten in.
It cannot be forced upon.
Nor even demanded from.
But is learned by example!

Lord, let me live the next five
minutes so that others may be tempted
to accept your love.

# OL' SWIMMING HOLE

When I was a boy and it was summertime and I wasn't perched on the counter of my grandpa's store, resting and listening, you could almost always find me down the road apiece, playing baseball.

If you came down to the pasture looking and didn't find a ball game going, then you would always know to follow a well-marked path that went on past where the right fielder would have been, under a barbwire fence, through a hollow or two, and beneath some thick bushes.

By that time, if you hadn't gotten lost, you would be on the bank of Big Black Creek, which is not the same as Little Black Creek, and you would surely be hearing a lot of hootin' and hollering. Then, if you just kept following your nose, you would be there. At my most favorite swimming hole of all time.

I remember once, when I had been a long time gone from that sleepy little town in southern Mississippi, waking in the middle of the night.

Dreaming that I was swinging on a rope out over that ol' swimming hole, and the water was black and evil looking and I was afraid to turn loose. Afraid to let go and drop into the deep, cold water.

I woke up with a scream gurgling in my throat and my clothes were soaked with my sweat and I could hear my Marine buddies in the closest foxholes whispering.

And I was sad.

That it had only been a dream.

But if you'd come looking when I was a boy and you'd found us there, you could have been a witness to the making of some of the happiest memories of my life.

Sometimes, mostly, we just shucked our clothes and jumped in. Other times we'd keep on our overalls since they mostly needed washing and it was fun to squeeze the air from your pockets while treading water. I can still hear the squishy sound and still see the bubbles erupting.

But then I went away. Nobody asked me if I wanted to move. I'm not at all sure anybody gave much thought to my feelings about the matter. There was a depression in the land and my folks were about as depressed as the next family. They didn't have much choice about it, either. Anyway, I moved away. But certainly not by my choosing.

I came back nearly every summer for a long time and I would light out for Big Black Creek as soon as my grandma made sure that I was all right. That I had actually survived another year in the city. She would check me over, from head to toe. Turning me first one way and then the other, talking to herself all the while. Looking back, I'm sure she was being amazed that her son-in-law had not let me starve to death.

Maybe it was the city living that was making me soft because every year the water would seem colder, and as I trotted along the path toward my first swim I would start shivering. Just thinking of the cold shock that would rack my body when I first hit the water was a pleasant sort of agony. And I would look forward to climbing out on the bank and to being warmed by the sun.

Those years when I was going back every summer it was almost as good as the years before.

Almost.

But then I moved again. A lot farther away. Besides, I was getting old enough to get a paying job when I wasn't going to school. Sometimes when I was. So I didn't get to go back as often, and I couldn't stay as long. So it changed. It wasn't the same. Know what I mean?

For one thing, I was well on my way to being a citified smart aleck by then and swimming holes without concrete bottoms, diving boards and girls didn't do a lot for me. Besides, there were boys around who didn't know me like my old friends, and I spent a lot of valuable vacation time proving that I was as mean and tough as I tried to act.

Finally the day came when I was back in that little town and didn't go near the ol' swimming hole. A part of my life had ended.

Just a little while back, I was passing through that part of my boyhood. The town itself did not seem much changed. The houses were older and there were some new ones. They'd torn down the old hospital that used to sit across from the lumber mill, right handy for all their accidents. And they'd built a new one about a mile away on the west side of town. Right across from the cemetery.

Before I could leave that day, I had to go and take a look at my most favorite swimming hole in all the world.

You're expecting now, aren't you, that I found a shopping center in that pasture where we used to play ball? And a superhighway slashing across the fields and my Big Black Creek swimming hole gone forever? Right?

Wrong.

Not yet. Maybe never. Oh, there were some changes. The cows seemed a lot fatter than those scrawny critters that never wanted to get out of the way when I was chasing a pop foul.

But Big Black was almost unchanged and the swimming hole was still there.

I sat on the bank, alone, listening to the laughter of Bish and Cekar and Azzie, of Sam and Buttermilk and Ollie and Toxie. I heard the voices of playmates by the dozens.

The memories were bright and the day was good and I was glad. Even when time nudged me on down the highway, I was happy that I had bothered. To go back again. To remember.

Learning once more that while remembering is often painful, it is also a way of my celebrating life.

My life and my memories.

Thanks to my God.

# SEED OF NEW LIFE

"It has been quite some time
since I have written, but I think
of you often."

When they brought him out to see me, that first time, John was wearing the same sort of dirty-white coveralls that all of the prisoners in the county jail wear. His had not been washed in some time. Neither had John. Both smelled of old sweat. And worse.

John's hair was wild and uncombed and he needed a shave. His eyes were dead and buried in his pale, expressionless face. They looked at me, the eyes did, but gave no sign of seeing. He was almost like a zombie.

The jailer told me that he was in a catatonic trance. That either he would not or he could not speak. Sometimes, as I talked, it seemed he was understanding me. Mostly he just sat there. Once or twice he wept, without making a sound. Just big tears easing out of those dead eyes and running down his grimy face.

They said he had been that way ever since he'd been transferred there from the city jail. Where he had been taken when they arrested him. For trying to kill his eleven-month-old infant daughter. In a fit of rage. Brought on by jealousy.

He wasn't quite twenty years old, still a teen-ager.

"It is ever present in my mind . . .
the kindness and understanding that
you showed me . . ."

Once a week, for more than a year, I visited with John. We had long, deep conversations. Well, mostly he listened while I talked. About life. And death. And God.

Mainly, I kept saying that God loved him. That He was offering him forgiveness without any conditions. No strings attached.

Seeming to regain a measure of emotional stability, John began asking a lot of questions about a lot of different things. But always coming back to his daughter. Did I really hurt my little girl? How could I hurt my little girl?

Then one day John was not there. One of the other prisoners told me about it. He had been improving every day, had become more rational, and so he was given regular privileges. Including the privilege of shaving.

Standing at the wash basin, in front of the mirror, John had calmly cut his throat. Without a sound.

> "I want you to know that
> my life has completely changed."

When he finally returned from the hospital and regained visitor's privileges, John and I started all over.

His stroll with death obviously had given him a new willingness to look at himself and his life. And his relationship with a strange God.

Somewhere in the midst of our weekly sessions, John was tried and convicted and sentenced to twenty-five years for his crime. By that time, though, he had discovered his new freedom. He had accepted the love and forgiveness offered by God. He was ready to take the social consequences for his heinous act.

Before being shipped out to the state penitentiary, he asked for two things. That I find out for sure that his daughter was all right and in a good home. She was. And that he be received as a member of the Church. He was.

> "You planted a seed . . . and now
> it is blooming."

For several years, John and I have kept in touch. On a spastic kind of basis. I haven't written as often as I would have liked, but still enough that he's been aware someone remembers. Someone cares.

Even so, his last letter came as a surprise. A pleasant shock.

It came with his annual Christmas card. But not from the state prison. It came from a little college town in another state. Someone told me that it is a beautiful place, with rolling hills and lots of trees. A quiet, peaceful place.

The letter will always be one of the nicest Christmas presents I ever received. Knowing that John, already given new life by his God, is now getting another chance from society to become even more the person God intended him to be.

> "I may not be the religious
> person that society would have me
> be, but I love my brother. I love my
> neighbor as surely as I love myself.
> And I love my God."

The message of the Gospel is in John.
That God is love.
That God loves you.
And forgives you.
And heals you.

# IS IT TOO LATE?

It wasn't all that important an issue.

But I blew my cool. Lost my temper. Exploded all over the people around me. That's the way it seemed to me later. That was the shame that came flooding and churning my insides.

Wanting to ease the pain of my guilt, one of you gently reminded me of the stress and strain that goes along with being in a position where your responsibility is to a lot of different people. Different people with different ideas and different demands.

For a little while, I bought that argument. I wanted to. Made it a lot less stupid if I charged it up to something or someone. Besides me.

But you know, and I know, that's a phony cop-out.

Maybe there's not anything that wrong with blowing off some extra steam. Letting some frustrations and aggravations get out in the sunlight where they shrivel and die. Needing gloom and darkness to survive. Maybe that's healthy.

But I don't have any right, God-given or otherwise, to do a single thing that diminishes you as a person. Righteous indignation may be acceptable, but unwarranted anger and self-serving abuse are in another category. Both are an abomination to my Lord.

And a hurt to my heart.

Thinking of my churlishness and wondering how to muster my courage to apologize, I was interrupted by a telephone call. Coming from a hospital.

While I'm here, you said, I'm taking advantage of my recuperating time to gather up some of the loose ends of my life. Maybe I won't tie them all together, you explained, but I'm pulling them out where I can look them over. At least I'll start working on them. Just in case, you implied.

Then you went on, explaining that I was one of your loose ends. That there were some things that needed working out between us and you were ready and willing.

Now maybe all our planning and dreaming won't ever get off the ground. But what's important is that you took that first step. You came across the barrier that was keeping us apart.

You showed me what I was looking for.

I wonder.
I really wonder what we wait for.

What keeps us fathers from having time to spend with our youngsters. From taking an hour or a day or a month—even forever—to listen patiently and lovingly while they do their best or their worst. To share what they are thinking and what they are feeling. Who they are and who they are becoming.

And what keeps you mothers. From being around when that always most important question wants to be asked. When that life-or-death advice is being sought and welcomed. When there's a pain inside that just needs to be eased. With a hug, a kiss, a special loving touch.

What keeps husbands and wives waiting until a better time to say, I love you. With the words. And the deeds.

What is there that dares to let us take a friend for granted. That lets us be indifferent to one another. That permits our self-concern to wipe out our sensitivity to the hurting of those around us.

Until it is too late.

🙰🙰🙰

When, O Lord?
When will I ever learn?
That my time is now?

# THE GREENING OF LIFE

A tiny finger of green pushes tentatively between the matted brown husks, is kissed by a brazen ray of sunshine ricocheting off an early morning dewdrop, and stretches hungrily for the nurturing love of new life.

Runty redbud trees, that yesterday stood with bared limbs shivering and naked trunks shrinking from the winter's vicious assaults, now promenade proudly with cloaks of purple rustling gently in a soft southerly breeze.

In silent suddenness fresh shoots burst the skin and greening twigs pimple the sleek complexion of the corkscrew willow as it joins the mass celebrating of new beginnings.

It comes like that. Silently. Almost unnoticed.

Unless you are looking for it. Expecting it.

And you are willing to stop in the midst of your labors. To take time to watch the grass growing. To smell a rose blooming. To feel the sun warming your body. To listen to the stirring of life.

An eerie stillness drifts by and settles over the land. Lingering. Sparrows, perched along the telephone lines, stop their incessant chattering and swing silently, uneasily. Dogs quit barking and slink under houses and bushes. The neighborhood toms abandon their eternal quests and streak for home.

As though embarrassed, the red-faced sun ducks behind the velvety blackness of a blustering cloud bank that comes swaggering out of the west. Spoiling for a showdown.

For a few brief moments as the tension mounts, it's almost as though the whole world is afraid to breathe and stands with heart thumping and temples throbbing, waiting for the worst. It almost comes.

Pouring out of the sky with relentless fervor and rattling a thousand and more roof tops, two-inch hailstones come drumming, cascading like BB pellets across the good earth. Bruising the new-born grasses, the budding flowers, and battering the still dormant plants.

The violent barrage ends as it began, only to be followed by rivers of rain slashing wildly at the fragile trees, digging ugly trenches in the newly laid flower beds.

Sometimes it comes like that. With such sound and fury that the sense of being is assaulted, outraged.

Unless you take seriously the signs of the times. And you are willing to let yourself be ready.

For whatever.

The story of spring is that and more.

It is affirmation of Easter and reaffirmation that we live beyond Easter.

Spring is new life coming into being. As quietly and as miraculously as the caterpillar shedding his cocoon and swapping his earth-bound clumsiness for the soaring grace, freedom and beauty of the butterfly.

It is new living breaking out of old habits. As raucously as a titillated bluejay. With all the force and magnificence of a mountain stream bursting its banks in joyous celebration of melting snows merging with warm spring waters for the nourishment of the thirsty plains.

Whether heralded by the comforting calls of the katydids or by the howling of tornadic winds, spring is the glorious wonder of a God-sized miracle. Witnessed to by the greening of the world, refurbishing and rejuvenating its resources to face again the insatiable demands of mankind.

Easter then is that God-sized miracle that gives meaning to the greening of life.

The tiny blade of new grass lives because the seed for its life was given and protected by those dead, matted husks.

The butterfly is, but only when the caterpillar is not.

I am.

You are.

We live. But not just because He died. But because He died and now He lives.

How strange, I wonder, that for all of its glory, spring soon grows faint and falls victim to the merciless heat of summer.

What about you? And the greening of your life?

# RISKING

If you're gonna go out climbing mountains, you've got to be prepared to face the danger. Of falling off. Or maybe even being pushed.

When this thought struggled out of a crevice where long ago it must have slipped and become wedged, it was quickly joined by a pointing finger.

While the finger was wagging itself in front of my face and counting cadence, an inner voice was rapping out an accusative question. So that's why you're not that much on climbing? Whether it's mountains or tall hills or on top of the house.

By now, you've already become aware that this isn't exactly a new problem with me. This matter of me risking myself. It is a continuing, raging battle that goes on inside me.

Mostly now I have good feelings about my personal relationships. My willingness to share me with you. And my willingness to accept your sharing you with me.

But not always.

That mountain can be frightening.

Yet, when we have stripped away all the façade, it may be that climbing that mountain is the most important aspect of our life. Risking our personal feelings is basic in all we do.

The man who would dare to seek the Presidency of our country and the woman who would serve as an elected public official put the same emotions and feelings on the line as the young boy telephoning that cute little red-haired girl for the first time.

While presidential aspirations seem on top of the highest peak around, the truth is that it is traumatic for many of us to initiate a relationship. Of any kind.

One thing for sure.

Whether it's finding a date for the sophomore hop, trying to carry on an aggressive program in business or in church, or seeking ultimate power—there is risk!

You can avoid that danger.

You can guarantee your safety.

You can stay off the mountains. The hills. Even that slight rise in the road ahead.

Yeah, you can.

You can also be walking around dead.

# NOT YET, LORD

Listen.

Somebody out there has got to help me.

It was only a little while ago, surely not very long, that I stood and watched him leave the house one morning. It was his first day of school and my heart was permanently lodged in my throat.

For he was a little lad, small for his age, a "cotton-top," with hair closely cropped and light blue eyes that came alive when he mustered a timid smile from his elflike face.

He was going hesitantly. Not too sure it was the right thing, for the town was new and the kids were all strangers. But he came home after a while with a new friend and a new zest for schooling.

But now.

Now there's a conspiracy around. Trying to make me believe that it is time for him to leave home again. And this time for college. To begin studying so he can become a psychologist. Of all things.

How can that be?

It's been such a little while since he was a fourth grader. He rode the bus that year for we were once more in new surroundings. Living out in the country and having to go to school with total strangers, he could have had a miserable time.

The first week, I remember slipping off and going up to the school to see how he was making out. I would park across the road and kind of slump down in the car seat so I could watch him during recess.

We've laughed about it a lot. As the smallest and the newest kid in his class, he had three fights the first day. After that, it was smooth sailing. Nothing but friends.

It was in that semi-rural setting that we first learned of his extraordinary powers of concentration. Having one brother too old and another too young for close comradeship, he invented a one-man baseball game.

All it required was one of my golf balls and the concrete steps leading up to the church. He played it incessantly, wearing out dozens of golf balls, reducing the side yard to a dust bowl, and amazing the whole community with his fierce competition. Against a well-known enemy. Himself.

Listen, I don't care what those letters say. The ones that keep coming from the director of admissions at that high-falutin' university over on the Atlantic Coast. It hasn't been any time at all since he was starting out in another new school. This time in the sixth grade.

We had moved at the beginning of summer and about the first week, someone came around to sign him up for the baseball program. Only ten years old, he'd already played three years on organized teams and somehow the folks in the new city had found it out. Probably because his daddy talks a lot.

Anyway, that was a short while ago. It was the beginning of a new phase in his life. That amazing ability to concentrate began impressing his teachers and he was moved from one honors program to another. Meant more study. But more learning, too.

During those years and the ones that have come scrambling after, pushing me aside and hastening on their way, I wonder if he has really known about my love for him. My inordinate pride in him.

Watching him gathering academic and athletic awards in those years when he was stretching his mind and his body. When he was becoming a gangling 6′ 3″ and the pride and joy of the Honor Society, my pride in him kept pace.

Not just for his accomplishments, though they are certainly impressive, but because he is as he is. And that in a strange and wonderful way, I am part of the miracle that is him.

And now. Now that I've taken time to think about it, it is very right and meet that this young man stretch himself once more.

It is time. Time for him to spread his wings and to reach out for the sun and the moon and all the peoples that on earth do dwell.

If I die a little bit when he is leaving, it is only just. For in him, I will be living even when I am dead.

Ah, but there is a burning of tears behind my eyes and the desolation of my heart is denying my words.

It's not really time, is it?

It was just yesterday when he came home. Bouncing and laughing, and hollering.

Daddy, Daddy, come and meet my friend. He's in the first grade, too!

∽∽∽∽∽

O God, don't just fill my heart
with those memories. Grant me strength
to stop my tears. That I, too, might
walk boldly into your future. Alongside
all my sons.

# AN ANONYMOUS FRIEND

I don't remember the first time I saw him.

One Sunday, it just dawned on me his was a familiar face. One that I had become used to seeing without even being aware. Because there were always so many people, maybe, but also because he was just not the sort who stood out in a crowd.

Smaller than average. Elderly, but not ancient. Wearing a neat but rumpled sort of look. Know what I mean? Hair always freshly trimmed but never quite combed. Suit that needed pressing, but not much. White shirt clean and fresh but already wrinkling, and tie insisting on being a little bit askew.

It was months before I found out his name. He would manage somehow to slip away before I could find him. When I would buttonhole some of the old-timers and describe him, they had to confess they just didn't know him.

One day, finally, I made contact with him. Discovered he lived alone. In one of those hotels for senior citizens that are best described as havens of loneliness, custodians of despair.

Meeting him, I learned that he wasn't the least bit strange. Just quiet and shy and lonely. God, he was lonely! So started a strange and beautiful friendship, lasting for several years and including long, philosophical conversations. Adding to my understanding of life.

They called me when he was admitted to the hospital. Just for tests, they said. But maybe you would like to come and see him anyway. He would like that.

Walking into that freshly starched room, my heart did a nose dive. Lying in that bed, outlined against the crisp white sheets, he seemed so small, so forlorn, and somehow I knew he was dying.

As we were talking, I began feeling better. His bright, still twinkling brown eyes kept denying the depth of his pain. His dry humor put me at ease and I was able to relax, making our time together pleasurable.

I told him then, for the first time, and I'm glad that I did. Told him that he reminded me a lot of my daddy. That he looked and talked a lot like the way Daddy had looked and talked. And that Daddy had been a loner, too.

So then we talked about fishing and hunting. Made a solemn agreement to take ourselves an outing when he was able to be up and around. And when the weather could be depended on to warm us.

Come to think of it, it was me that did most of the talking while he did the listening. And dreamed his dreams and thought his own thoughts.

When I left, I was planning to visit again the following day.

And I did. But only to touch his cold face. To whisper a final good-by. They told me he died quietly in his sleep. Slipping away in death as he had lived in life. Without anyone noticing.

So he's gone now and not many people knew him well enough to grieve.

Not the young nurse who is even now realizing her lifetime ambition. Because my friend, learning of her dream, made the money available for her to go to Africa to work in a mission hospital.

Nor the teen-ager who was able to have desperately needed dental surgery because someone told him of her accident and he responded.

And not even the hundreds of youngsters who have a place to live and three meals a day because he long ago gave the bulk of his fortune to the orphanage supported by his church.

That was the way he wanted it. That was the way he was.

His giving and his helping were never so the world would hold him in high esteem.

Like another Man, he did what he did because there were always people in need. Who were hungry. And cold. Sick. And in jail.

Knowing him is some kind of blessing for me.

I wish you could have known him.
But, maybe you did.
Or, maybe you will.

Thank you, Jesus, for letting
me know my friend. For opening my
understanding with the beauty of
his gracious love.

# MOUNTAIN TOP

Coming down off the top of a mountain is not something I like to do. Nor is it something I am able to do casually.

Whether it happens while pulling a camper-trailer down the narrow, winding trails in the Smokies.

Or whether it's slipping and sliding feet first through the rocks and thorny brambles of the Chisos Mountains in the Big Bend country.

Or when it is taking leave of the warmth and fellowship of a retreat to come back down into the valley where the telephone jangles and the traffic snarls and the crowds are impatient with waiting.

One summer there was a special mountain top.

It was a working retreat and I wasn't overly enthusiastic. Getting away from routine and frenzy is usually welcome. But not when it means substituting a new routine and a different kind of frenzy.

So it was with reservations that I agreed to go and to be the director. To be in charge. Lord, how easy it is to lead me down any old primrose path. Just a few ego strokes and away I go.

But I'm glad I went.

The mountain top became extra special the first night as I sat out on the grassy slope with a visitor who had driven hundreds of miles to see me. And surprise me.

We sat silently a long while, watching the deer feed. In close communion with the stars and the bright moon and the floating clouds. And each other.

We didn't talk a lot, my son and I, but our thoughts were walking together and a fresh new bond of love began to grow.

Between us.
And with our God.

With that unexpected gift came many others. The always thrill-
ing discovery of friends, some new and some not.
One who sings with the voice of an angel, makes heavenly
music on the piano, and warms the world with his cheerfulness.
One who declares his faith with humor and gusto, who challenges and dares and invites.
One who works quietly and efficiently, always with a suitable
suggestion. The right word in the proper place. And no pretenses.
And dozens more who worshiped with a different sort of zest,
who were more willing than not to share their love of Christ.
Openly and freely.

It is tempting.
To want to stay on the mountain. To want to build there a
booth for protection from the rain and the cold. And just stay.
To help protect me from that temptation I have this prayer:

> God, renew my desire to face once
> more the valleys of life, where you spend
> your days. Feeding the hungry. Healing the
> sick. Visiting the lonely.

Which is all well and good. Most impressive.
Except I've been thinking.
What's keeping me from those same mountain-top experiences?
No matter where I am!

# THE CHANGE

She has been coming to see me for months. Mostly to talk about and to complain about the loneliness of a big city. Or to inquire about other job openings. Sometimes to take off her mask. And to wonder in pain if her life is ever going to be anything other than a long, boring television romance. Constantly interrupted by commercials.

Plain looking she is, with a drabness that is always identified with cheap and ill-fitting clothes. A dreariness of appearance linked and bound to an outlook of indifference.

Until just the other day.

I had not seen her for several weeks and when she came walking into my office I honestly didn't recognize her at first. The change is startling. Almost amazing.

Wearing a smart new outfit that even smells expensive and bubbling with a contagious happiness, she's like a newly minted coin. All bright and sparkly and eager to be mixing and mingling with the world.

Asking her would have been silly and a waste of time. She was telling me all about it before she had gotten inside the door. There is a young man. A most special young man. From her home town. He had come to the city especially to find her and to tell her that he loves her. And wants to marry her.

One day, maybe, there'll be an epilogue to this tale. Hopefully it will have the sort of ending that will offer a warm fuzzy for you and for me.

For the moment, though, I'm going to be satisfied if the story itself serves to help both of us recognize an often-forgotten, but well-known truth. That both our outlook on life and our living look are dependent on our knowing that we are loved. And on our accepting that love!

Learning that someone treasures you is the beginning of the miracle that changes you from a frog to a prinz. Letting yourself accept the gift of love completes the transformation.

The wonder of such magic causes a glow that starts on the inside and works its way through the layers of your rejected feelings. Until it finally surfaces.

For all the world to see and to marvel over.

And talk about.

For me, there is something about knowing and accepting that I am loved that is nearly indescribable. A being-satisfied-with-creation sort of feeling that seems to start out with a tiny tingling and spreads until the bells of Adano are vibrating the world with the good news.

The knowing is the first sip. A wee taste of what can be. Of what may be. When the knowing is taken over by the surrender to and the acceptance of, that's when the human soul explodes with celebration.

When love is accepted.


Could it be?

That we are happiest during the Christmas season because it is then that all the sights and the sounds are reminding us.

How much we are loved.

By our God, who is love.

Who sends His message.

By a baby born in a manger.

Born that you and I might live.

With the knowledge of our love.

And willing to accept that love.

Because it is given. No strings attached!

# OUT OF MY DIARY

This is not something that I do easily and casually. This revealing of some of the hidden thoughts of my aloneness.

I am moved to do it. I am enabled to do it. Because you are my friend. You are special in my life. And I need your sharing in my intimacies.

Out of my diary.

This is some kind of day. Brand new. Bright and shining and all sparkling. Wearing a hand-painted card that says, From me to you, with love. Signed God.

The day started early. Blew in on a strong wind that sent garbage cans clattering down the alley and had me shuffling through the house in the darkness, closing windows. Tempting me to slip outside and to stand, shivering, exhilarating in the sweet freshness of God's breath.

And there to be grabbed by the unbearable loneliness of man apart from his fellows. Then to be rescued by a warming awareness. That being apart from does not mean being separate from.

In the middle of early-morning darkness and surrounded by the uncomfortable stillness of a suburb at ebb tide, feeling a sudden presence. Knowing, in a rare flash of intense emotion, that I was sharing my experience.

With you. Through the miracle of love.

God's.

And ours.

I got barefooted tonight and walked in the grass. With my toes I could feel the individual sprouts and the squishiness of the lawn that had just showered in the evening's dew.

Breathing deeply of the sharpening breeze, I took the time to observe and to be impressed by the stars standing watch at the edge of space. Ready to sound the alarm in the event of an unwelcome intrusion.

Trembling from the cold and inner excitement, I watched tiny goose bumps parading on my bare arms. Wondering where they came from and where they went.

Stepping unexpectedly on a sharp rock, I discovered an equally unexpected joy in the midst of the pain. In the recognition that where there is feeling, there is life.

So I celebrated life.

My life and yours.

With God.


I was walking along a remote beach this morning when the fog became so thick that it was frightening and I was more than a little uneasy. So I stopped and sat on the wet sand, waiting for it to lift.

Watching the forboding mass drifting across the water. Feeling its moist fingers sliding along my face. Hearing the constant rumbling of the waves rushing toward me and the incessant crying of the sea gulls as they organized their fishing.

It seemed to me that time had frozen.

That eternity had opened and swallowed life.

In a moment of absolute clarity, I knew that man's survival is a continuing tribute to the greatness of God.

That the power of His love and forgiveness overwhelms my despair, my loneliness.

Whenever I am open to Him.

Whenever I am open to you.

P.S.

It would be good if I could tell you that the sun came breaking through at the moment of my feeling of at-one-ness. But it didn't.

When I trudged slowly back along that lonely beach, the fog still seemed to blanket the world. It could have been a gloomy, scary walk.

But it wasn't.

It never is.

Not really.

# CHRISTMAS MORNING

Stabbed awake by some mysterious inner timing device that defies my understanding, I swing my legs over the side of the bed and sit there a moment. Groggily. Stretching, I'm aware of the early morning stiffness of joints that goes along, I keep telling myself, with an active middle age. Then, in the predawn bleakness I remember the day and a tremor of excitement begins to stir me.

It's Christmas morning!

Quietly gathering my robe and the old blue scuffs that should have been thrown out a long time ago, I slip from the bedroom and go padding down the hall. Musing: so it's Christmas, you nut, what are you doing out of bed? The children are older now and we were all up late last night. It'll be hours before anyone else even stirs.

Oh, well. I'm awake, so I might as well be up. Putting on a pot of coffee, I go out to see if the morning paper has come. Didn't really think it likely. Young men who throw a morning paper route have to make their rounds early all right. But not that early. Besides, looking for the paper was only an excuse to get outside for a few minutes.

It is really great. Gratefully real.

There's such a freshness in the cold air that I find myself wondering aloud if the angels had stayed up through the night to wash and polish the atmosphere, getting it ready for this special day.

To the east, a faint light is beginning to reach aggressively across the horizon, stretching strong but graceful fingers to bring life and order out of the chaotic shadows of the night. The frost-covered grass, brown and lifeless the day before, sparkles now with the promise of unborn vitality.

Far overhead, hidden under the soft night cover, a flock of geese offers a background of wild primal music, orchestration for the miracle of birth.

Shivering in the cold, I'm in awe of the beauty of that moment in the new day that my God has created. In the universe of my heart there is jubilation for the love that brings life to a beginning. And a hallelujah chorus celebrating the birth of that love.

It's Christmas morning!

Back inside, the coffee is perking cheerily and the fire, hastily lit when earlier I passed through the den, is burning merrily. Despite all that happy commotion—the cheery perking and merry burning—everyone else is still asleep.

The good wife is cuddled under her electric blanket. The middle son, home for the holidays, sprawls catty-cornered across a double bed. Looking at him, I marvel. Yesterday, it seems, he was hardly long enough to fill a crib. The youngest one has kicked off his covers and is curled in a knot. Hard, brown muscles making a mockery of his being the "baby."

Across the hall, behind a door slightly ajar, come the easy sleeping sounds of my beautiful daughters. I tiptoe lest I wake them. Especially the blonde who is past voting age and college-trained to sleep late.

In the den, still another sleeps. Lady MacTavish, our grande dame Skye Terrier. This is her thirteenth Christmas and she wheezes and groans and whimpers. Maybe dreaming of earlier days when smaller children filled her stocking with their candy and cookies.

Get your rest, old girl, for today will be long and busy. In a little while, the quiet will be gone. The house will rock with music and the babble of voices, laughing and talking. And the insistent shrilling of the telephone. The wondrous invasion of the older children and the grandchildren.

There'll be a throbbing of life and our hearts, responding to the excitement, will pump harder and faster. Across the whole world there'll be new awakenings. To the miracle of His birth, His love, and His new life.

Yes, it's Christmas morning.

Because God is loving the world, loving you, loving me.

It is Christmas.

The day that marks the gifting of God. Packaged in love. Wrapped in life.

O Lord, break the quiet of my
sleeping heart with the joyous celebration
of the birth of new living. In Jesus.
Amen.

# LISTENING

To awaken to the steady beating of a pulse that just a few hours before had fluttered and pounded wildly, prompted by the panic of the strange hospital room and fueled by the irrational fear of dying alone in the dark.

Then to listen once more to the whispers of breezes touching and telling while still hiding behind the fog wrapping the early sun in a misty veil.

To look out the window again and watch a leaf turning slowly to that sun's first warmth while lazily shaking off the lingering drops from the night's shower.

Discovering with ever-renewing amazement the marvel of new life emerging out of a dead past, of a new growth budding from old roots, of fresh and exciting vigor suddenly thrusting past discarded dreams.

Fiercely exulting in the joy of being.

That comes from listening. To the message of life.

And knowing that I am loved. By you. And God.

And knowing that I can love also. You. And God.

A wise one said, There is nothing new under the sun. And it certainly isn't original when I tell you that it takes a special kind of love to be able to share yourself. With another person. With God.

It takes a depth of feeling that is almost as hard to describe as it is to possess. Maybe you can call it love. Or call it trust. Call it faith. Call it whatever you will, it's a scary risk to lay open your heart. To let your secrets filter into the light of day.

Especially when your pride and confidence have leaked out of the cracks caused by the ruthless hammering of an insensitive husband. By the incessant nagging of an unhappy wife. By ungrateful children. By parents who don't understand and don't care.

And when your worthwhileness has been destroyed by deliberate manipulations or by indifference born of neglect and nurtured by apathy.

It surely takes a depth of something or other to muster the words to talk about your hurt.

It takes a great courage to risk one more rejection. Another back of the hand across your raw ego. It takes understanding God's love, for me to be able to share with you.

But there's something else. Something that I'm guilty of forgetting.

It takes a special love to listen. And to hear.

God knows that maybe the greater love is in the careful, hurting hearing. Of your wife. Of your husband. Of your children. Of your parents.

The kind of listening that is not impatient to interrupt with a defensive denial. Or an angry reply. Or a soothing solution. Or even a comforting directive.

But the sort of listening that is tuned to my problem and my agony and my despair. That maybe doesn't have any answers, but acknowledges me.

Love it is that offers a listening heart.

And with infinite capacity wraps me gently and carefully in pools of concern. Washes away my aches and pains even as the ocean's waves ease the sand castle into nothingness.

Listening and sharing.

Maybe the one is taking and the other is giving. Yet there is in them a loving sameness.

Depending on where I am. Where you are.

Depending on our hearing the message of life.

And on our listening hearts.

# INSTINCT

Maybe it was my conscience bothering me. Or it could be an indication of the mileage on my personal calendar. For whatever the reason, I was up and puttering around at a ridiculous hour.

I don't know the exact time because my clock was not awake. But I can tell you this, it was too dad-blamed early. If I had the sense that the Lord gave to a peanut, I'd have still been in bed. All curled up and warm as a frankfurter at a wiener roast.

Instead, I eased out of my bed while it was still pitch-black, stumbled to the kitchen to start the coffee, and discovered that under the cover of darkness a raw day was creeping up on the world.

The wind, while not yet howling out of the north, had worked its way up to a loud whine. There was a feeling of winter in the cold concrete as I barefooted my way down the front sidewalk in search of the morning paper, not yet arrived.

About to go back inside I heard a strange, yet familiar sound. Somewhere above me, hidden from sight by angry clouds starting to boil, a flock of geese was flying south. Listening to their anxious conversation I was first concerned whether they would safely navigate the village skyscrapers.

Then I was envious.

How great it would be to be able to follow the seasons. One day to be at home in the canebrake of a Canadian lake and to feel the first whisper of an icy breath on the back of your neck, and the next day to be traveling, with family and friends, toward a warmer climate.

What freedom, I thought, not to have "things" that cannot be left behind. Not to be rooted by responsibilities. Not to be anchored by attitudes and prejudices and the opinions of others.

In the midst of this early morning heresy, I was caught by a nearly uncontrollable shiver and I hurried inside.

Was it just the cold?

Or an inner struggle that I will not admit?

Well? How is it with you?

Back in my comfortable and familiar old den, being warmed by a cup of freshly brewed coffee, there came a second thought that needs sharing.

Watching as the layers of darkness gradually peeled away to reveal the bleakness of the day, as pellets of rain began splattering against the picture window and sliding eagerly toward the waiting soil, I was overwhelmed by the harshness.

Every instinct in me yearned for a fire in the open fireplace and all my family gathered round for conversation and food and games and warming, loving fellowship.

Looking out upon the grayness, an oppressive blanket settling down on the outside world, I longed for the security of staying at home and being nurtured by familiar comforts and the closeness of family.

Can it be, I wonder, that man is innately and eternally an agrarian? Is it possible, despite our conversion to urban life with its concrete jungles and all the technological marvels, that we are farmers at heart?

That our instinct will always be to stay at home and cuddle with a fire when it is too wet to plow?

Obviously, I'm not approaching this subject with scientific expertise. Have no intention, for example, of doing a lot of research with in-depth interviews, diverse sampling and all that other stuff that is commonly used by serious students.

I'll leave that to you.

But I know how it is with me.

When the weather is bad, my instinct says stay home. When it first starts getting cold, my instinct says fly south.

Something tells me that's the way of living. Now. And then. Whenever.

It just isn't all that simple and easy.

〰〰〰〰

Lord, let me be wise enough to
enjoy my living in this complex age.
Strong enough to claim my share of
your responsibilities. And free enough
to share myself with others even as
you give yourself to me.

# WHAT'S YOUR CHOICE?

Being awake and stirring around while waiting for the sun to come nosing into a new day is not exactly my favorite pastime. On the other hand, for one reason and another, I'm no stranger to those particular circumstances either.

In the Marine Corps, for example, it was just one rude awakening after another. Most all of them while the sun was only a promise. Starting with those (deleted) cold showers that were part of my boot camp torture. Progressing to five-mile cross-country runs while training in the wilds of Oklahoma. Then being routed out before dawn to wait, to eternally wait, for orders to move up. Or back. Or sideways. Somewhere.

And how about all those mornings I spent in duck blinds? Shivering cold and wet bottom and legs cramping. Wishing to the Almighty that he had given me enough sense to spend my leisure hours doing something else. Anything.

Don't forget when I was too young to know any better. Delivering a morning paper kept me groggy and sleepy most of my youth. And for some strange reason I was always starting off on camping trips in morning darkness. Same thing for getting to the county fair every year.

Spending a few days on the Coast recently triggered memories of those early risings in bygone times. Likewise causing me to remember a lesson learned long ago. And so often forgotten.

Each morning during that vacation stay in a beach home facing the east, the rising of the sun was an adventure in beauty. A splendiferous display of God's incredible artistry. While the image, for me, is always just a thought away, I decided to try and capture it on film. To share with others. And to help me remember when my days are growing cold.

Wanting to preserve the full beauty of those first tiny streaks of orange fire surfacing from the dark waters to stain the gray-blue horizon, I rolled out of my bed while it was still dark as the inside of a whale's belly. Stumbling over sand dunes and bits of broken sea wall, I made my way to the beach with my camera.

Picking a spot that would enable me to use a picturesque driftwood log in the foreground of my photos, I hunkered down on the sand and waited for the sun to come up.

And waited. And waited.

Shivering there in a damp breeze that suddenly came whipping across the rolling water, I remembered.

It takes a long time for the sun to rise. When you are impatient for it to happen. When you are anxious to be on your way. When you are wanting things to get started.

The light is a long time coming. When you can hear the ducks but still can't see them. When droning engines serve warning that enemy bombs will soon be falling and your gunners are straining to see in the darkness.

Waiting for the sun to rise is waiting for light enough to see where you are going. Whether it's down the creek bank where the trot lines are tied. Or around one of life's dangerous curves.

I've got to keep remembering.

If seeing the sunrise has top priority, then patience is needed.

If getting on with it is more important, I'll simply have to learn to stumble in the dark for a while.

And there are times when I can only do one or the other.

O Jesus, quicken my heart to let me
know when to sit patiently waiting for new
light. And when to risk stumbling in the
dark of my blindness.

# REACHING OUT

It happened somewhere back down the road aways.

Some event or some person or something just flat rared back and hit me right between the eyes with an insight. Stopped me dead in my tracks. Got my attention long enough for the idea to take hold.

This is my show and tell.

Wanting you included in the dynamics of my living involves more than my being willing to reach out to you. It means my taking on the responsibility for our relationship.

Whatever it is.

Whatever it becomes.

Let me try to explain.

Experience keeps making me painfully aware that my reaching out does not always and automatically produce positive responses. No way. Maybe because my reaching is clumsy or overanxious. Maybe you're just not ready for me. Maybe you are hurting and not wanting, not caring to be included.

Whatever.

When that happens, as it often does, my responsibility does not end. Possibly it increases. For now it is important that I accept your negative response. Recognizing it is not always a rejection of me as a person. Letting it be a learning for me. By dealing with it openly and with as much reality as possible.

If I'm not willing to be that responsible, I can destroy our relationship. Easily. By saying and doing only those things I know will create your positive response. By using phoniness to manipulate your emotions. By prostituting our genuine relationship in an irresponsible effort to appease. It's not very honest.

But it is easy. And popular.

One of the reasons I'm always catching myself not living up to my own understanding of responsibility is fear.

Often I'm afraid that the ties that bind us together are too fragile to stand the stretching of honest differences. Of genuine emotions.

Or I'm afraid that maybe I'm not yet enough of a whole person to walk away unaided from a collision of principles. That my maturity isn't up to that kind of testing.

Or I'm afraid your self-assurance is so tenous, your self-image so tentative, that any hint of disapproval or disappointment will bring your world crashing down in flames of insecurity.

Which is to say that I am afraid you will not understand the depth of my love. Or that my own feelings of rejection will blind me to the certainty of your love for me.

Yes, I have. I surely have. And many times.

Thought about drifting aimlessly and rootlessly along my way. Without ever becoming too involved with you. Just being satisfied with a superficial, game-playing relationship.

It is the simplest way. The easiest.

If only I didn't keep remembering.

The one who is ever reaching out His life.

Including me and you and whoever.

And not standing in the wings, waiting to see how we are responding.

Just reaching out.

Lord, please keep challenging
me to risk my living by loving.

# STRANGE

If I had been born a hundred years sooner, give or take a few, I know how I would have ended up. I wouldn't have liked it, but I would have been a mule skinner.

I can just see me now.

Slumped in utter boredom on the iron-hard seat of a bumpy Conestoga. Reins hanging limply in one hand. Taking a swig out of a jug with the other one. All six horses barely clomping along, heads bowed in the desert heat.

Stretching out on the prairie behind me, an endless stream of wagons. And ahead? Nothing but more wagons. And horses' derrieres.

This wagon-train image came flashing across my screen one morning while I was locked into the expressway traffic. Being held up at nine o'clock by all the eight o'clock commuters who were stacked in behind the seven o'clock crowd.

Long as I was there and didn't have anything better to do, it seemed like a good time to tell you about a strange thought. And how it came about.

This is how I put it into my little recorder.

Woke up early this morning.

Heard geese talking as they passed over. Wonder where they started from. Where they're headed.

Got up and pulled down the windows. Got back in bed and pulled up the covers. And drowsily marveled at the miracle of the changing seasons.

How would it be, I thought, if God had arranged it differently? So that it was summertime all the time, everywhere? Or winter forever?

What if it stayed day continually? Or night?

Feeling warm and snug, but still tingling from the brisk chill in the early morning air, I would vote right now for a never-ending fall. Mild during the day and sorta chilly in the evenings. That's what I really like!

But for how long? Before I would be yearning for something different. Something to stir my blood. A storm of rain and lightning and sleet and ice to test me. A burning hot day to give me appreciation of the difference.

I keep trying.

But I just don't seem to find a way to improve on God. And his creation.

Isn't that strange?

# LANYAP

Scuppernong brown and butterball round, I remember sitting on the counter in Grandpa Bishop's country store. Bare heels beating a tattoo against the sturdy wooden supports, drops of sweat rolling down from my armpits. Leaving crooked little roadways across the layers of dirt and grime.

Wearied from hours of baseball in the merciless summer heat of my southern Mississippi boyhood or plumb tuckered out from rassling with ol' Buttermilk Risher, a sometime buddy and that depending on who was whipping who, I would often seek refuge in the relative coolness of that small frame building. The economic and social center of the community. Of my universe.

Here it was that I first learned about a strange custom.

Whenever a family came in from the country to shop it was an important occasion. A happening. Both for them and for my grandfather. For all of us, I guess.

Settling the preliminaries never took very long. The lady came with her mind made up. So much sugar and flour and spices. So many jars for preserving and a large bottle of rubbing alcohol for the old man's rheumatiz. And don't forget that patent medicine that cures everything, besides making you feel good in the process.

Then would come the haggling over the price of dress material. The agonizing selection of ribbons to make bows for her bonnets. Adding a mite of flavor to everyday drabness.

Almost always, before the bargaining was settled, she would look longingly at the loaded shelves and the barrels of merchandise, drop her eyes and say, Mistuh Bishop, what sort of lanyap y'awl got for me this time?

Mostly it was a small sack of hard candy, sometimes a yard

measuring stick, once in a while a can of snuff or a plug of tobacco, depending on whether the wife or the husband did the deciding.

But always there was some lanyap, a little something extra. Something more than what you paid for and could rightly expect. Something that was in appreciation of you.

You can see, can't you, how fascinating that could be for a nosy kid. You know. The sort we've learned to call inquisitive youngsters today. I was always intrigued by the exchange and became fidgety and impatient waiting for Grandpa to offer his lanyap.

Looking back, I know that old gentleman was some kind of man. Even if he did wear a beard and let his hair grow long in the back. The folks who owned their places and had money usually received candy or trinkets of little value. Those who cropped on shares and barely made it one year to the next were apt to get extra food or cloth while each of their children were presented a bright stick of peppermint candy.

It was a long time before I learned that the lanyap of my youth is really lagniappe and had its origin with the French Creole merchants who were the earliest settlers in the Gulf Coast area.

And I hadn't given it a lot of thought one way or the other until the other morning. When I woke up before the sun and enjoyed a time of letting my thoughts wander aimlessly through the memory banks of my time. Remembering those days of my precocious youth, I was suddenly caught up. Not by the lanyap of my grandfather's store, but by the lagniappe of my now.

Like the fresh love of a little girl who comes daintily across the room, picking her way through a noisy crowd, climbing up on a chair and wrapping her arms around my neck. Something extra!

Or like the lady banker whose dark, twinkling eyes reflect an inner beauty and a loving spirit. Who takes the time and effort to share her gifts. Something extra!

Oh, but you know how much lagniappe there is for me.

The way your eyes caress me across a room, the touch of your hand when my nerves are raw, cross-country telephone calls from children venturing the unknown, the friend who is finally paroled from prison, the black man who calls me brother and means it, the woman who smiles through her tears and says, You've helped me know God. The love of so many, the trust of those who want so desperately to trust. Something extra and extra special for my living!

But what about you?

Anything extra in your life?

# LETTING GO

A scorching dryness seared the roof of my mouth. My hands, nervously twisting, were soaked in sweat born of fear. A queasy sickness slowly churned in my stomach. My heart's wild thumping pounded, pounded, pounded in my ears.

I was, in every literal sense of the expression, almost scared to death!

Like it was yesterday, I remember it. But it happened a long time ago. Way back, when I was ten or maybe eleven. At the annual county fair. Seeing, for the first gut-grabbing time, the daredevils who ply their trade high above the madding crowd. The trapeze artists.

Afraid of watching. More afraid not to. With each pendulum movement of the sky swings, my fear mounts. Until the climactic leap through space jerks me out of my seat and to my feet, panic-stricken. Screaming. Dying inside and being reborn when the landing was safe.

It was about ten years later that those same feelings returned. And then some.

Climbing awkwardly and painfully down a rope net hanging over the side of a Liberty ship rolling and tossing in tempo with the waters of the angry Pacific Ocean. Glancing fearfully at the tiny landing boat as it bobbed and bounced to the tune of a different drummer.

When I yell JUMP! that's when you let go, the sergeant had said. Just be sure that you push out or you'll wind up very wet, he had added. And slightly dead, he could have said!

There are a lot of things that can be said for Marines. Both pro and con. One of the pros is that they mostly learn to follow orders. To do what the man says.

I did.

I let go when he yelled. And I pushed out, and I landed safely. Because ol' sarge knew what he was doing, and I trusted him. Trusted him enough to turn loose. At the right time.

It's been growing on me through the years that learning to let go is one of the most difficult things we do in this life. Whether floating through the air on a flying trapeze. Or standing with tears in your eyes when your child drives off to college. Letting go is hard! It is frightening, and it is hurting.

Please. Please don't get the idea that it is something that comes naturally. That we can just automatically do. Fact is, we come into this world equipped with a pair of grabby hands attached to arms inclined to wrap around and to hang on.

Hanging on for dear life is the old saying. For sure death is more to the point. For sure, slow, suffocating death.

A child is learning to trust when he learns to jump into your arms. From a chair, then from a table, and finally from the side of a swimming pool. Each leap is a leap of faith, made with the simple trust that you will catch him, lest his foot be dashed against a stone. With every venture, the love existing between you grows. And grows.

Isn't that what learning to let go is all about? Love? Loving that is deep and strong, trusting and fulfilling.

When I am open and willing for loving to be the essence of my living, no longer am I devastated by the never-ending demands that I let go. That I let live.

A case in point. For me and for you.

When the girl-child who just a little while ago needed her hand held while she crossed the street, when she is suddenly a woman full-grown and full-blown. With love in her heart and marriage on her mind and motherhood in her dreams. When she has reached that plateau and your pride in her and your love for her are overflowing.

Then, darn it, you let go!

And she has a new and different life. And you are more whole, while less than you were!

And it hurts. Oh God, how it hurts!

But how much more if you can't let go. If you hang on to yesterday when tomorrow has come and gone.

Lord, scrape from the smallness of our souls those
instincts that smother and stifle the love of those
whom we love. Teach us, O gracious Master, to let go.
To turn loose and to celebrate the freedom of our children.
Amen.

# TWO SIDES

When I was a tadpole trying to survive long enough to become a regular frog, I didn't have much of a halo. And, now that you ask me, I still don't.

But in those bygone days, I had a certain reputation. Came by it honestly most likely. To most of the mothers in that little ol' saw-mill town that was my home, I was a roughneck. Always fighting. A shame and a disgrace. Well, that's how they saw it.

You'll understand then this technique that I developed and used. For example, if I was tusslin' with ol' Buttermilk Risher and he went home crying, I'd light out for my house. Hit the porch with bare feet slapping dust from the pine boards and hollering at the top of my voice. Crocodile tears splashing all over the place, I'd claim that I had been jumped on by Buttermilk and about three others. All of them bigger than me.

What I was tryin' to do was save myself a whipping when Buttermilk's ma showed up, as she surely would. Indignant. Mad as a wet hen locked out of the chicken yard. Demanding that I be taught a lesson. That I needed paddling worse than a boat floating down a river toward a waterfall.

Really, it wasn't a bad technique. Mine, I'm talking about.

What happened afterward, though, depended on a lot of things. Mainly on who was home when all these histrionics were being enacted.

If it was my daddy, he'd ask only one question, "Did you whip him?" If it was my grandmother, she'd hold me in her arms and say, "Where are those bullies? I'll skin their hides for picking on this baby."

But if it was my mama, I was in trouble. Deep trouble.

Well, what did you do to him? she would ask. And why? And who started it? What about? It wouldn't take her long to get at the truth. Which was not always in my favor.

Hardly ever.

In recent times, my recollections of that particular game and the ways of all the different players have brought some insights to mind.

It reminds me again that each of us has our own particular way of looking at things. And that way is influenced by heritage and relationships and exposures.

My daddy didn't give a hoot for the right and wrong of kid fights. He figured that would even out. What he wanted was to be dead certain I took up for myself. And for icing on the cake, he wanted me to be the best fighter in town. It was that simple.

On the other hand, I was the apple of my grandmother's eye and could positively do no wrong. Where she was concerned, there was never the slightest doubt. I was her little angel. Picked on by the bigger kids and maligned by all the mothers in town.

It was my mother that was the real problem. She wasn't disturbed by and didn't care about the fights, either. But what she kept putting in front of me was my need to face up to what was real. To acknowledge what was the truth. And to change my behavior with my growing understanding.

Any of that sound familiar?

Something else.

It was true then and it is true now. Whether in little-boy fights, or marital conflict, or national furore, or religious controversy.

There are always two sides.

And, in my understanding, neither has all the right. Nor all the wrong.

But let's be specific about that for a minute or two. In the Church, God's Church, we are ever witnessing an agonizing fight. Sometimes pitting brother against brother. Parents against children. And husbands against wives. Friends against friends. Until the divisions are dividing the divided!

I do not, and neither can you, claim that any one side has all the right. Or all the wrong.

But I do believe.

With all my heart.

That the gospel of love calls you and me to a more important mission than self-destruction through internal conflict and eternal bickering.

Lord, open all hearts to the beauty
of your love. Let the honesty of our
living proclaim your good news to all.
Even those who are so dear. And so distant.
    Amen.

# GOING HOME

The huge jet is starting to descend through heavy layers of clouds. Straining to see through the swirling gray mass that seems to be pressing clammy hands against the plane's windows, I am suddenly conscious of unusual inner tension.

Partially, my uneasiness comes from a feeling of being smothered by those angry clouds. But only partially. Probably a lot less than I want to believe. The overriding cause grabs me and shakes me roughly as that flying hotel breaks into bright sunshine. And there, stretching out before me in all her glory and grandeur, there is the land of my birth.

I am going back home and almost there.

How much has it changed, I wonder? And me?

Hot and humid and as ill-tempered as the day itself, I sat squirmingly on the hard wooden bench. Squeezed between Grandma Bishop and my Aunt Ruby, I think it was. Unable even to wiggle around enough to catch sight of any of the other kids, I gave full attention to a dirt dauber building a house without hands in a place where the warped boards no longer came together. When he dived out of the screenless window to fetch more makings, I concentrated on watching the preacher's Adam's apple. You ever do that?

Sometimes I'd snicker. Right out loud. And then my aunt would give me a dirty look and squeeze my arm hard. Probably just as hard as she could, and it was always my pitching arm. Then she'd whisper loud enough for the whole congregation to hear. Hush, boy, or ah'll tan yo' hide good when we get home! You hear?

I remember once, after such a Sunday morning, my grandma took me by the hand and we walked through the old cemetery that was out behind the church. As she led me through that silent place, she pointed out the graves of our kin and she would tell me how they had lived and how they died. Then she would look at me and say, Someday, boy, we'll die too and then we'll all be together again.

Boy, she would say, that's gonna be a glorious day!

I had come home, back home. But can you ever? Really go home again? Go back again?

I walked again in that dusty little town, smaller than I remembered. Everything smaller, it seemed. And I wandered through the same little graveyard, yearning to hear once more the voice of my grandmother. Yet knowing with all the logic and reason of my maturity, that her voice is stilled forever. Buried in a pine box, six feet under the grass where I stood. Laid to rest so many years ago.

Perhaps. Perhaps the sound of her voice has been stilled. But not the memory of her words. For I hear them, comforting and loving when I am lonely and afraid. And I still feel her great arms catching me and holding me close to her bosom when life's hurts had come crashing through the barriers of my childhood.

I still hear her contagious laughter, and I never stop feeling the endless love and patience of an old woman for the boy I was. A boy seldom good and never for very long.

With the jet still climbing, I caught a glimpse of that great river, muddily snaking its way to the Gulf. And took a last look at the place of my beginning.

I'm glad I made the trip. That I went back home. Decades of memories had come crowding in, all clamoring for attention and being jostled aside by the next familiar face. By still another long-forgotten escapade. Old times dead but not forgotten. Hooray, hooray!

But now there's a new excitement that has me looking out the window. Searching for landmarks. A lake up to the north. A freeway over yonder. Discovering familiar sights that tell me I'm almost there. That I've really come home! Back to my now! Where I live and work and play and pray and have my being.

Bringing with me, as I always have, my heritage. Unable to

leave any of it behind. But never being buried by it either. Not able to separate myself from what was bad while hanging on to all the good. But refusing to let my future be absolutely controlled by my past.

Knowing there is a now that seeks my alert and creative attention, even as there is a past that is worthy of respect and inspection.

Knowing.

As my grandmother did.

As my grandchildren will.

Knowing there is reason and purpose in living. In loving. In dying. In Christ.

ᖇᖇᖇᖇᖇ

Lord, warm us with the love of those
saints who have gone before. Freshen our
todays and quicken the fires of our
tomorrows.

# NOW GO TO SLEEP

As a grandparent who hangs around with a number of similar types, I consider myself an expert witness.

The cute sayings of children are often not. And it doesn't necessarily matter whether the grandchild is part of my brood or belongs to someone else.

Sometimes the sayings of children are dull. And boring if repeated too often.

Once in a while they are tragic.

This story was passed along because a lot of people consider it to be hilarious.

The mama is the source, and her delight in sharing the incident is obvious.

It seems that she overheard her three-year-old daughter getting her doll ready for bed. The little girl had patiently dressed the doll in pajamas and carefully tucked her in her own little doll bed. Mama then heard her precious baby.

"Now don't you worry," she clucked, "everything's going to be all right. Your mama's right here. Jesus loves you. Your mama loves you. And if you don't go right to sleep, I'm going to beat the daylights out of you."

Maybe. Just maybe. A casual reading might evoke only a chuckle. Maybe a little tch-tch. A fleeting thought that small children are like sponges, absorbing all the sounds and fury of life. Without really understanding. Without really being affected. Without any harm. After all.

God. O God, forgive us!

I don't have to be a psychiatrist or a psychologist to be terribly appalled by the conflict of influence that is being indelibly imprinted in that child's memory. That is already affecting and afflicting her thinking. And her behavior.

On the one hand given warm assurances of love. By a mother who hugs her close, protects her, tucks her in bed, making her know that she is special and loved. By a Jesus who is pictured as a friend. A kindly, beautiful young man who has a special and protecting love for her. For children.

And then.

By that same mother? Or by some other person close to the heart and mind?

By someone! Threatened with a beating unless she close her eyes and go to sleep on command. Unless she stop that endless chatter. Unless she get out of everybody's way. So the party can start. So the fun can begin.

Come on a time journey with me.

The year is 1998.

For all my fears, that little three-year-old made it.

She survived. Now she has two children of her own. One by the boy who got her pregnant when she was fifteen. They did get married but, like everybody said, it didn't last long.

Her other child is by her second husband. A little girl. She was born a month or two before the divorce was final. And she's never even seen her real daddy.

Still, you know, the mother is doing better. She's gone through a couple of breakdowns. Not really mentally ill, you understand. Just not able to cope emotionally with the world. With life.

Afraid to trust people who say they love her. Bitter about a Jesus who was touted as her Saviour by someone who beat her and scolded her and slapped her and said iloveyou.

Can't understand it. Can you?

Oh well, not any use worrying. Life just keeps on keepin' on.

Heard her laughing the other day. Telling a girl friend about a cute thing she overheard her little girl saying.

Seems her little daughter was putting her doll to bed and . . .

∽∽∽∽∽

O God. Forgive us.
Beginning with me.

# PERSPECTIVE

Seems to me there was a time when I did a better job of keeping things in perspective. And it wasn't nearly as big a job as it is now.

Back when I was collecting Indian-head pennies. Sneaking into the picture show on Saturday nights to watch Hoot Gibson and Tom Mix. And dreaming of growing up to become a real big-league baseball catcher like Mickey Cochrane, or maybe ol' Bill Dickey. Back then I didn't have to spend a whole lot of time figuring out the priority of events in my life.

For example.

If I rolled out of my feather bed in a winter morning's darkness and the pine floor was colder than a well digger in Alaska, the alternatives were clear-cut.

I could jump back in bed, knowing good and well that my mama would shortly be after me with a hairbrush, or I could freeze slap to death almost while jerking on my overalls and running tippy-toed into the kitchen to cuddle with our old wood stove.

Mostly that's what I did. Freeze slap to death almost. But sometimes I would stubbornly take my chances with the hairbrush. Which meant that I would wind up with a bottom warming and the rest of me freezing. Which was a lot of help in the development of my perspective.

In a like manner, with the first really warm day of spring the options were as plain as could be. I could play hookey, qualifying for a double whipping but momentarily gaining a new lease on the whole idea of living, or I could go miserably to school. Dying a little with each step. Then suffocating through the long, boring day.

It has been told about that I was a perspicacious youngster.

I played a lot of hookey.

Friend of mine whose only remaining daughter is being married started me thinking on this business of keeping things in perspective. On assigning proper priority ratings to events and things.

It seems to me that the whole world is having to adjust to this particular wedding. You know what I mean? Important things like golf and tennis and sitting around philosophizing with old cronies are being shamefully neglected.

Why, his total life style is being disrupted. Instead of spring baseball season and how the fish are starting to bite, he wants to talk about silver patterns and monogrammed linens. Disgusting! Maybe even immoral!

Luckily, I'm a patient man. And I know that as soon as the wedding is over and he's saved up enough money to pay off his bank loans, he'll be back to normal. Besides, I'm a forgiving person, and who else is there that's still willing to laugh at all my jokes.

Besides, if I'm getting around to being somewhat honest about this, I surely don't have any business fooling with the speck in his eye. Some of the nit-picking things that I allow to dominate my days are absolutely unimportant.

Getting our lives into perspective, and keeping them there, is never going to be an easy task. Mostly because we're constantly wriggling around like worms on fish hooks. Trying to hide what we're all about. Trying to convince someone, everyone, that we're better than we really are.

Else we're bowing and scraping and apologizing to the world for our intrusion.

Either way is surely an aggravation to the Creator. Who is most aware of our pimples and warts and blemishes. But who also knows that he made us unique and special and lovingly whole.

Maybe my perspective is as good as it ever was. Or better.

The problem being that it takes me longer nowadays to risk the cold floor. To turn left at that same old corner, instead of right.

To reach for that new lease on living. For that fresh breath of new life.

Instead of suffocating.

How about you?

# THE HURT OF BECOMING

Big Black Creek is a part of my history.

In those days when we weren't so industrialized and homogenized, its cold, spring-fed waters were fresh and clean. Ready for swimming, or fishing. Even drinking.

Wandering aimlessly through the thick long-leaf pine forests in my part of the southland, Big Black was my youthful companion. A trusted friend in my early adventuring. A keeper of hallowed secrets and a sharer of deep experiences.

Wanting somehow to share a special thought with you, I remembered the Big Black. Its waters churning past huge boulders anchored comfortably on a sandy bed. Slipping easily over a hidden log. So shallow in places that tiny minnows dart frantically about to keep from going aground. And at others, so deep that the water becomes dark and menacing.

In one of those pools, of legendary and unprobed depth, I learned to struggle for life. Literally.

I learned to swim. Suddenly and without warning.

Pushed into the deep, beyond the safety of the step-off.

To swim or to drown. Or so it seemed to me.

That happened a long time ago. But my remembering of it is vivid and alive. For it is part and parcel of my pilgrimage. A significant entry in the journal of my travels. A meaningful experience in my journeying to becoming what I am. And what I am to be.

Like all the other happenings of my yesterdays. And my todays.

This is my sharing.

That in our living we are always becoming. That through our

experiencing we are forever changing. Becoming more today than we were yesterday.

But there's much more.

When I listen to the hurt in your voice and sense the anguish of your flesh. When I am touched by the tragedy of your days, my compassion is real. Your hurting becomes my experience.

But that is not enough. Not enough.

The love that is in me, because of knowing I am loved by Another, is more than being open to experiencing your hurt and your anguish. Your tragedy and your broken heart.

That love must also be able to recognize and survive the helpless knowing that there is nothing I can do to keep you from hurting. My love must include a willingness to live with this shocking truth.

For in a deep and honest sense, love does not mean taking the pain of another's burden. No matter how willing we are. No matter how frustrating it is to stand by while your child, or friend, or even a stranger, struggles for survival in a deep pool of problems.

Love is knowing.

And accepting.

And living with the reality.

That growing comes with experiencing.

There is one thing more. It isn't likely to change your hurting. Not really. But you know that because of my love, you are never alone in your suffering. And your becoming.

He makes possible my love. And yours.

# OUT OF THE MOUTH . . .

He's only six years old but I can already tell. He's got all the earmarks. He's really gonna be somebody. Probably an All-American football player. Or a Rhodes scholar. Maybe both. If he gets into business, he'll own half the state before he's thirty years old. If he decides on politics, he'll be governor before the turn of the century.

Of course, I may be a little biased and with good reason. He's the son of my oldest daughter, which makes my wife his grandmother. That means he's got some nice kinfolks.

In truth, he is a handsome lad, with deep brown eyes that literally dance with delight as he romps with friends and when he's thinking up some mischief. Which is often.

But there is another word for him.

He's unfettered. You know what I mean? A free spirit and an inquiring mind are his trademarks. Not yet and maybe not ever spoiled by irrational and illogical demands of a society geared to rewarding mediocrity so long as it conforms. To a system that, more often than not, rolls roughshod over genius simply because it is different.

Ah, well. Enough of the lecture. Let me get on with my story.

Recently Jack and his family moved into a beautiful new home and he was delighted. His room is upstairs, there is a park just down the street and, besides, moving is a great experience. With him, and most of us kids, experiences are the things that count the most.

However, in just a few days the moving bit got to be a drag. If he stayed inside, he was always having to tote and carry and hang up and put up and do all that junky stuff that Mamas are forever making poor little kids do.

On the other hand, going outside to play wasn't all that great, because none of his friends had moved with him and after you've ridden your bike up the hill and around the block about a hundred times or more, it gets a little icky.

Only slightly daunted, he poked around in the new garage and uncovered some left-over boards, a few nails, and a can of oil-base black paint. Eyes glowing with excitement and an engaging enthusiasm, he announced that he was gonna build an air-o-plane and he was gonna paint it black!

Mama was, as smart Mamas have always been, delighted. She was especially delighted that the project was planned for the garage, so he would be out from under her feet for a while.

But with one small reservation. Just a tiny one. No painting until Daddy gets home to open the can and help you stir it and etc., etc. OK? Okay!

That was some job. He started early in the morning and quit late in the evening. For three days. Hammering, sawing, grumbling about the stupid ol' nails, starting over, banging his thumb, yelling and crying. But never a thought to giving up. Showing a dedication unmatched since the Wright brothers had the same stupid idea.

Finally, it was finished.

All but the painting. So the waiting began. When will Daddy be home? In a little while. How long is that? Not too long. Aw, that's what you always say.

Thirty minutes seems an agonizing eternity.

Is he home yet? You know he isn't. Well, how much longer will it be? Why can't I just go ahead? Wait, wait, wait! That's all you'll let me do around here. Wait!

And then. Nothing. Silence. No more questions. No more impatience.

Suddenly the peaceful quiet becomes ominous. Concerned, suspecting, fearing, Mama hurries to the garage to check. You're absolutely right. He hadn't been able to wait. You are positively right. When he pried the lid open, the can tipped over and that beautiful oil-base black paint embraced hungrily the freshness of the spic-and-span garage floor.

And there was Jack.

Grimly and tearfully wiping at it with an old newspaper and his bare hands and his shirt and everything else in reach. Swallowing hard and biting her tongue, Mama showed him a better way to clean up the mess as much as possible. Then she spoke quietly to him of obedience. Worse, she reminded him that he would have the job of telling his daddy what had happened.

Daddy is quite a man himself. He let Jack do all the talking. Listening with gentleness and sensitivity. Then his lecture was brief and clear, without being too heavy. Though that garage floor is never going to be the same!

A few weeks later, Mama, under the pressure of running a household, serving as taxi driver for her children, and going to college two days a week, committed the unpardonable. After promising, she forgot to buy a toy that Jack had wanted for some time.

It was not until he came racing to meet her in the driveway, jumping with anticipation, that she remembered. To her ever-lasting credit, though she was dreading his reaction, she looked into his trusting smile and said, I forgot. I know I promised you, cross my heart and everything, but I forgot.

Then, God bless him, he put his arms around her waist and looking up with a smile, said, "That's all right, Mama. It's all right, 'cause I know why you and Daddy didn't yell and scream at me about spilling the paint in the garage."

"You do?"

"Sure. It's 'cause loving people is more important to you than garages and things. And I'm not mad with you 'cause loving you is more important than any ol' toy."

Isn't that what you always say?

# CALENDAR OF MY HEART

She's a real, living doll.

Flawless golden brown complexion. Blond hair with a tinge of honey hanging down past her shoulders. Dimpled cheeks and wearing only a saucy smile on her kissable lips.

The excitement of the day. The anticipation of a great adventure. And a built-in zest for breathing and talking and laughing and living are all combining to create a special radiance.

Reflecting a bubbling-over happiness with the whole idea of just being.

And why not?

She's six years old and today is the first day of school.

She's going to school! For the first time in her whole life. Oh, she's visited in the building a time or two. To get acquainted, you know. But that was only play-like. Today is for real.

You can almost see her hugging herself with joy, thinking about the magic of the day.

She was awake long before daylight. Lay there in the semi-dark, giggling and singing and shivering with excitement. And then. Up with a bounce. Washing her face. Brushing her hair. Putting on the special going-to-school dress that had been on layaway at the big store since early summer. Then the brand spanking new shoes.

Chattering away while barely touching her breakfast. Like her mama and her mama before her, talking a blue streak. About anything and everything. Then brushing her teeth, so many strokes up and down and so many across. A final brushing of the beautiful golden-honey hair. All ready, she announces with gusto.

And it's still an hour till time to go.

Oh, how long it takes for the big hand to make that trip all the way around the face of that old clock!

What time is it, Daddy? When can I go? Now? Please, Mama, now?

All right, off you go. But you be careful now. You hear?

And so she went.

Out of that little frame house. Down the dusty road that was Main Street in that sleepy little southern village. She went off to her first day of school, did my darling little daughter, those twenty short years ago. How well I remember!

And well I should.

For the big hand has made a full circle around the clock of time. Across the calendar of my heart.

This morning, a bright-eyed petite brunette. Skin a deeper bronze, like golden mahogany. Dark, flashing eyes and a smile that lights a room the way a torch shatters the darkness.

This morning, she went off to her first day of school. Did my darling granddaughter. Went laughing and giggling and whispering off into that great and exciting new world.

With her golden-haired mother standing in the doorway. Heart full. Remembering.

Remembering.

# MAKE A MIRACLE

Lord, where do I start?

There's such clutter and confusion in the files of my heart that I'm bewildered and frustrated. Maybe, Lord, if you'll straighten me out just one more time. Maybe then I'll be able to keep my life all neat and tidy.

Maybe.

Let's start with my friend of many years. Take him first, Lord. You know the one I mean. His days are becoming dry and dusty, scorched by boiling bitterness. Make a miracle, Lord, and carve the cancer of hate and hurt from his body and soul. Let your gentle love ease the emotional drought that has shriveled his feelings.

Touch deeply, Lord, the direction of his life's chart that he will once more cherish your gift of time. That he will be moved again to use your gifts for your sake. And his.

Then there is the young man who came just today. Who came and stood with his head bowed and whispered, painfully, Pray for me, please, pray for me. Remember, Lord?

He was a long way from home and alone. His father was dying and he wanted to go back. To be with him. But he didn't have any money. So he came looking for a miracle.

I'm a man, he said, with bottom lip quivering and little tears tiptoeing down the sides of his nose. I been to 'Nam and I come home. But now my daddy's dying and my mama's there all by herself. And I'm scared.

Lord, thank you for listening to us right then. Please, now, keep watching over him while he rides that bus and stares blindly out the windows. Give him the sort of faith he'll need to accept his father's death. Let him hold fast to the muscles of your love.

If it suits your plans, Lord, send him this way again so we can renew our friendship. And, please God, wipe from behind his eyes the fear of life. Somehow, help him to know and to accept that his blackness is only a color. Never a quality.

Then that little lady who's so special. And so sick. What sort of miracle dare I ask for, Lord? Maybe that she have less of the terrible pain that twists her body and tears my heart. And that her peace permit her to live each day hoping and praying to be cured. But preparing her each minute for dying.

And, oh God, so many others.

That man on the telephone who screamed and cursed and said he couldn't live any longer without his wife and children.

Yes, and the young woman who keeps telephoning and coming by. Confessing over and over that she is a murderer. Because long ago she was pregnant. And the baby didn't live.

Even, Lord—or maybe especially—that bill collector who is always taking advantage of my poor friends. Brow-beating them, persecuting them, and frightening them into paying two and three times what they really owe. Yeah, him, too.

And all people, Lord, who only go through the motions of living. Who are indifferent to loving.

For all of us, O Lord, cause such a commotion in our lives that we'll have a change of venue for our attitudes.

Give us a new birthday. Today. In you.

Make a miracle, Lord.

Amen.

# BIRTHDAY GIFT

Dear James,

Coming home from my trip a couple of weeks ago I remembered that some important people have February birthdays. People like Abraham Lincoln and George Washington. And you!

Then it hit me.

You're going to be sixteen years old this next week. How can that be?

Just a short while back you were four going on five and my severest critic. Maybe you've forgotten. It was in the little church where I started out preaching and your mama used to make you sit on the front pew with her.

Man, I can still hear you. Every time I preached longer than five minutes, which was mostly always, your loud sighs of boredom kept things interesting. Causing the ladies to look at your mother indignantly, while their husbands just sniggered. You were something else.

And how about that day, it doesn't seem that far back, when you hit home runs the first two times at bat? Both times, when you had finished racing around the bases, you came over to the wire backstop, shouting loud as you could, Did you see that, Daddy, did you see that? You were just eight then and home runs were new.

Sturdy as an oak stump and tough as a pine knot, you played your first year of organized football in a league made up of eleven- and twelve-year-olds. That was the year you were nine. I used to slip off to watch you practice, my heart in my throat and my body aching from the punishment you took from the older and bigger boys.

But you had to play. And I guess I had to let you.

You've played a lot of games in the last few years. Football and baseball and basketball. Even some golf and a little tennis.

Guess I've seen most of them. At least, I've always been there when I could make it. Not that you ever made a big deal about it, but it did always seem important to you. That made it important to me.

A lot of other memories, James, come tumbling across the years. Our summer camping trips, swimming in the Gulf, climbing mountains in Colorado, exploring in the Big Bend, the endless table games, corny jokes, and rainy nights under leaky canvas.

Sixteen years old?

In a lot of ways, son, you are much older. You have always taken your share of responsibility. Working to earn your walking-around money, and even to buy most of your school clothes. Standing up for things you believe in and being loyal to your friends. Recognizing that school is for education. By your concern for your environment and for the people who share it with you.

I know I don't have to tell you, but I want to. You're just great! Like your brothers and sisters, but different. Along with each of them, you are unique and special in your own way.

That long drive home, James, was a good time for thinking. Out of my thoughts I have selected a few memories to remind you of what has been. Only a few of my feelings to let you know what is. And but one insight to what will be.

Time, son, is a birthday gift.

But it cannot be saved.

It will not allow itself to be hoarded.

Does it not seem to you, then, that it is to be lovingly and wisely spent? Given over to creative, joyful and essential living?

Out of my experience, I testify to you that time becomes far more important when it is past, than when it is.

Not only on your birthday, but on every day of your life, I have given and continue to give you my love.

But I cannot give you time.

For time is God's birthday gift.

May he also give you his understanding so that you may accept and cherish and celebrate his gift.

Love,<br>
Dad

# LADY MACTAVISH

The hour is late.

A sudden wind whips through the branches of the trees and low-lying clouds are moving swiftly. Sometimes blotting out the stars. Sometimes not.

Shivering, I stood quietly in my back yard, watching with tear-blurred eyes as my husky fourteen-year-old son stuck a shovel in the hard ground and began to dig.

I kept shaking a little. Remembering a lot.

It was thirteen years ago and our family was new in this part of the world. We'd left our ancestral home and migrated west. There were seven of us. Peggy, that's the wife and mother, and me, fifteen-year-old Pam, eleven-year-old Mike, six-year-old Bill, and the baby, eighteen-month-old James (then called Butch).

The seventh? That was Pepper, our Boston terrier and a recent addition to the family. Really, a concession of sorts to make moving more palatable.

Remember the trauma involved in moving?

The breaking of old ties and the fear of having to start all over in building friendships. We had our problems but, in the midst of them, we were making it all right because we had each other. You know what I mean?

Then, only a few days after we had gotten settled in our new home, Pepper disappeared. For days we scoured the neighborhood, knocking on doors and furtively looking into back yards. But either Pepper had been dog-napped or he had gotten homesick and lit out for Mississippi. We never saw him again.

Imagine the cheeriness in our household. Everybody spoke in monosyllables. Meals were rehearsals for a wake. Gruesome.

As James stepped back from digging to rest, I took up the task. It was a good feeling, driving the shovel hard into the dirt, straining to deepen the hole.

But it only made my memories sharper.

I remembered the afternoon, those thirteen years past, when a curly haired, tail wagging Skye Terrier came frolicking into our family life. She just wandered into the yard and refused to leave. Fearfully, we ran an ad in the local paper and checked with the missing pet bureau. Each night, when the telephone would ring, everyone would be terrified. Afraid that her rightful owner was calling to claim "our" dog.

But nobody ever did.

We named her Lady MacTavish, but she was never called anything except Mac.

And I kept remembering a lot of other things. A lifetime of happiness with a little dog that adopted us. She chose us, I'm convinced, and spent her whole life making sure we knew this. That we understood and accepted her love and faithfulness.

And how she was always too fat and what a ridiculous sight she was, romping in the yard with the children, trying to get into their football games and always the first volunteer for after-dark hide-and-seek sessions.

Smiling, I remembered how her long hair covered her eyes and the bad jokes that strangers invariably made, about whether she was going or coming. It was a mark of her kindness and good will that such boorish behavior never bothered her.

There was one thing that she detested. It was having her thick wool cut. About twice a year we would take her to the vet and each spring she would come home with a "crew cut." Out of the car she would jump, into the house she would run, and under the couch she would hide. Ashamed! How like a woman.

I had long since wearied in the digging and my son was doing most of the work. It's too dark for me to tell if he has let himself cry. If he hasn't, I hope he will.

I hope he'll let himself understand that it is all right for a man to cry when there's a hurt inside and an aching that needs the therapy of tears. Only a boy in years, he's a man in a lot of ways.

You can be sure that he grew up some tonight. When he and I buried the little dog that had been a playmate and a friend for most of his life.

Later, when the night sounds were stilled and the others were sleeping, I went out again to say my personal farewell. To give my God thanks.

Standing in the quiet, awed as always by the endless stretching of creation across time and space and life and grace, I could only wonder.

About how different our living would be.

If people, and starting with me, were as faithful to their calling as the good Lady MacTavish.

# THE WORLD IS COMING TO
# A BEGINNING

Lord, it's so good to be alive! To feel and smell the mint crispness of your early morning breath. It's exciting to stretch my arms to your sky, to be kissed by your sun as it slides over the roof tops on its way to work.

Sitting out on the front steps, Lord, watching the miracle of dew soaking new color onto the cheeks of grass grown wan with winter, I am overwhelmed by the awesomeness of your fresh creation. How does that grass grow, Lord? That spider, up under the roof, how does he spin his web? How does my heart beat and the blood and life keep pumping through my body? Oh, God, how great you are!

Thank you for this new day and thank you for the love that sends me zinging into the living of my life, eager for the experiences made possible by you. Ready for the choosing which you leave to me.

Oh, it's great to be alive, Lord. I thank you again!

God, help me.

You remember when I started out today I was so excited. Ready to climb a mountain, or swim an ocean, to go off tilting with windmills.

But now, Lord, I need your help. My gut is all in knots and hurting. Not a stomachache, Father, but deeper, like I'd been drinking acid. You know what I mean?

The young girl who came to talk to me about an abortion. Remember? She's barely fifteen years old. Not even in high school, and she was acting so hard. So indifferent and uncaring. So I'm pregnant, so what? That's what she said. Oh, I know that deep down she was scared and crying, not really believing this was happening to her. That's part of my hurting, I guess. Not knowing how to get beyond the mask of her feelings. Just being so helpless when she needs so much help.

And the lady out at the nursing home? You know the one I mean. Let her die, Lord. Please let her die! I remember, as do you, when she could feel and think and smile and cry and hurt and see and be. But now—O God—now she's just not! Please, please let her go.

Lord, there's a lot more. It was quite a day.

The man who called to let me know the job I told him about was already taken when he got there? He's a good, hard-working, honest man, Lord, but he's getting desperate. His children are hungry and his hope is dwindling. Prop him up, Lord, and make him aware that he has a place in your world. That he is worthwhile, as a man and as a father. Help him. Through me. Or somebody. Let him find work!

There's still another thing, Father, that's tearing me up inside. It's making me doubt myself, sapping my strength and resources even as the day stretches and yawns into the night.

That's the hurt that I caused my friend. Believe me, I didn't know that I was being hurtful, but I was. I know I was, because my friend loves me enough to tell me.

And that makes me wonder, Lord. How insensitive am I, if I can hurt so deeply and not even know it?

That frightens me. How many others have I been hurting in the same way? Who don't care enough to tell me? How often, Lord, have I hurt you by failing the people in my life?

Lord, I know you forgive me and I am grateful, but please give me a greater awareness so that I may not fail so often, so the aching will be less, so the hurting won't last so long.

God, help me!

Lord, it's quiet now.

The house and everyone else in it are asleep. The only sounds are the creaking of windows and the gentle snoring of people and cats. And the dripping of a faucet.

I wanted just another minute or two of your time. To thank you for the goodness of your day. To say that you've made me feel your love so that I'll rest well in the night, looking eagerly to your next new creation.

And what I'm most thankful for, O Lord, is that in you our world is always coming to a beginning!

Amen.